Math

MARIO
CA...MUSTO

TEACHER TIMESAVERS

Published by Scholastic Publications Ltd,
Villiers House,
Clarendon Avenue,
Leamington Spa,
Warwickshire CV32 5PR

© 1992 Scholastic Publications Ltd
Reprinted 1992, 1993, 1994

Authors Marion Cranmer and Catherine Musto
Editor Margot O'Keeffe
Sub-editor Jo Saxelby
Series designer Joy White
Designers Lynne Joesbury, Clare Brewer, Joy White
Illustrations Gloria, Hilary McElderry
Cover illustration Frances Lloyd
Cover photograph Martyn Chillmaid

Designed using Aldus Pagemaker
Processed by Pages Bureau, Leamington Spa
Artwork by David Harban Design, Warwick
Printed in Great Britain by Clays Ltd, Bungay,
Suffolk NR35 1ED

British Library Cataloguing-in-Publication Data
A catalogue record for this book is
available from the British Library.

ISBN 0-590-53003-8

Contents

Teachers' notes   5

Level 1

Sets   11
Bags of apples   12
Dominoes   13
Sweet boxes   14
Lollipops   15
Pattern repeats   16
Flowers   17
Heaviest/lightest   18
Classroom shop   19
Morning routine   20
True or false?   21
Snakes   22
Make a pattern   23
Shapes with cubes   24
How many sides?   25
Where?   26
Piles   27
Toys for sorting   28
Belongings   29
What might happen?   30

Level 2

Halves   31
Three-digit numbers   32
Number cards   33
Difference pairs   34
Money track   35
Guessing handfuls   36
How many?   37
Look-out towers   38
Making 10   39
Colourful towers   40
Jumping frogs   41
Ribbons   42
How far up the jar?   43
Measuring strips   44
Units of measurement   45
Shape friends   46
3-D structures   47
The maze   48
Finding the way   49
Shoes   50
Free choice   51
Is and is not   52
How likely?   53

Level 3

Link amounts   54
Cold days   55
Travelling by train   56
Making a tables game   57
The birthday party   58
Buns for bears   59
Rolling dice   60
Fill the jar   61
Lose or gain?   62
Pencils   63
PE teams   64
Looking for patterns   65
Programmed   66
Mr Mystery Maker   67
The digital clock   68
Boxes   69
What could you use?   70
Guess the weight   71
Shape sorting   72
Cut and sort   73
Buried treasure   74
Structures with cubes   75
Cinema visit   76
Favourite day   77
Colours   78

Level 4

Chocolate pieces   79
Bigger and bigger   80
New uniforms   81

Which number?	82	Use your head	107	Train journeys	132
Possible products	83	Make it big	108	Value for money	133
Stock check	84	Nextdoor neighbours	109	Tessellating shapes	134
Can you calculate?	85	How close can you get?	110	Tessellations	135
Sharing the bill	86	Triangles and squares	111	Robot	136
Matching the pairs	87	Find the formula	112	Designer tiles	137
Square numbers	88	Plotting	113	Mini-man and Maxi-man	138
Starting numbers	89	Co-ordinates	114	Measuring heights	139
Mystery picture	90	Openings	115	Guest speaker	140
Plotting shapes	91	Packaging	116	Spoilt for choice!	141
Gold blocks	92	Snail trace	117	Throwing	142
Plasticine weights	93	Flooring	118	Twins	143
Cubes and cuboids	94	Congruent shapes	119	What are the chances?	144
How much time?	95	Tourist	120		
Angles and lines	96	Stop the waste	121		
Pyramid	97	Television times	122		
Rotating shapes	98	Recipes	123		
Logo designs	99	Favourites	124		
Rotation	100				
Happy birthday	101	**Level 6**			
Snacks	102				
Watching television	103	Decimal numbers	125		
Totals	104	Jolly jumpers	126		
		Sam's Bistro	127		
Level 5		Decimal fun!	128		
Drawing to scale	105	Sequences	129		
Powers	106	Soap powder packets	130		
		Production costs	131		

Introduction

This book is not offering a schematic approach to teaching mathematics. It is a collection of individual tasks that provide opportunities for the children to use and apply their knowledge of mathematics in conjunction with other mathematical materials and resources.

On page 10 a grid is provided to show to which attainment target each activity relates. Each activity addresses a statement within a particular attainment target as indicated on the grid. However, statements from other attainment targets may be covered depending on how individual tasks are developed. Due to the investigative nature of the activities, aspects of Attainment Target 1: Using and applying mathematics, are implicit in all the tasks.

The activity sheets may contribute towards evidence of a child's level of attainment but should not be the only means of assessment.

Organisation

The children should work autonomously and build on their previous experiences, reinforcing aspects of mathematics already covered. The sheets are not to be used as unsupported introductions. The amount of preliminary discussion necessary has been left to the professional judgement of the teacher.

Children may work alone on the activities, although some involve data collection and may benefit from collaboration. The benefits of preliminary and follow-up discussion with the teacher and/or other children must not be forgotten.

The teachers' notes should be referred to before the activity sheets are handed out.

❑ Denotes ideas for extension activities.

Level 1

Sets (AT2) The children could draw the sets rather than stick them into their books.
❑ Try to reverse the order of the cut out sets, starting with the set containing most objects and ending with the set containing fewest.
Bags of apples (AT2) The children may use buttons or counters to match to the apples in each bag. For those who have difficulty cutting out, use a set of 0-9 cards. This activity is best copied onto card.
Dominoes (AT2) The children could sort the dominoes for the different totals of numbers of spots. How many spots are there on their set of dominoes? On a double five set?
❑ Hide a domino from the set and ask the children to work out which one it is.
Sweet boxes (AT2) The aim is to make sets of ten. For some children it may be appropriate to match buttons/counters to the sweets.
❑ Explore making 10 using three different combinations. Zero should be included.
Lollipops (AT2)
❑ Ask the children to draw a given number of extra lollipops. They could also sort them according to shape and colour.
Pattern repeats (AT3) The children may notice that some examples of the pattern can be broken down into shorter sections. If unsure whether the child is really repeating the pattern, let them continue it further.
Flowers (AT3) Explain that, when making a different pattern, a linear arrangement is still required.
❑ Include a different type of flower.
Heaviest/lightest (AT4) A selection of objects suitable for weighing needs to be available in the classroom.
Classroom shop (AT2) Some children may need guidance when pricing items, to ensure that

they stay within a number range in which they can operate fairly confidently.
Morning routine (AT4) The pictures may need to be changed for some children.
❑ Comic strip stories are a good source of pictures for cutting up and ordering.
True or false? (AT4) This activity encourages children to examine printed information carefully. It gets away from the most commonly asked question of 'which is heavier?' Encourage them to explain how they know the answers.
Snakes (AT4)
❑ The children could make Plasticine snakes that are the same length as the paper snakes. These could then be curled up to use to find out if the children understand conservation of length.
Make a pattern (AT4) The children may choose to use the pattern pieces to form a random shape or to reform the original shape in a different arrangement. It is useful to have an outline of the original shape to work with.
Shapes with cubes (AT4) Encourage the children to look for duplicates in their collections of shapes. Discuss whether some shapes are the same or different.
How many sides? (AT4) This activity helps children to concentrate on the number of sides rather than the name of each shape.
❑ Go on to make shapes using straws, geostrips and other construction apparatus.
Where? (AT4)
❑ Encourage the children to think of other prepositions to illustrate. They could be used to make a game such as Pelmanism.
Piles (AT5) It does not matter how the children choose to sort the pictures as long as they can explain their reasons.

Toys for sorting (AT5) Encourage the children to observe similarities and differences. Some children should just sort the actual toys and record their attempts by drawing their sets.

Belongings (AT5) This activity could be done with clothes or toys belonging to the children.

What might happen? (AT5) When drawing their own pictures the children may include activities such as going to school, staying at home, going shopping and going to the park. They should be encouraged to think about what influences the likelihood of what they do, for example school holidays and weekends.

Level 2

Halves (AT2) Discuss the fact that halves do not necessarily look the same and that there is more than one way to halve each shape.

Three-digit numbers (AT2)
❏ Include 0 as one of the numerals. Allow each numeral to be used more than once.

Number cards (AT2) If possible, copy this page onto thin card. Make more cards if required.
❏ A simple game could be a useful way of using the cards after they are completed.

Difference pairs (AT2)
❏ Using number lines or hundred squares, colour the numbers where the difference is 4.

Money track (AT2)
❏ An element of probability (AT5) could be included by asking questions such as 'If there is no time limit, will you pick up all of the coins?'

Guessing handfuls (AT2) The main focus of this activity is to encourage children to estimate. Stress that estimating or 'guessing' is not about getting the 'right' answer every time.

How many? (AT2) Draw attention to the fact that children can usually pick up fewer bigger things than they can smaller things. Why do handfuls of the same toys vary in number?

Look-out towers (AT3) Bricks of the same size should be used. Draw attention to the numbers of bricks that built towers of equal height. Do they know that they are called even numbers?
❏ Predict the answers for a number above 20. Predict the numbers of bricks that would build 3, 4, or 5 towers of equal height.

Making 10 (AT3) Encourage the children to estimate how many more they require each time. Record results on squared paper.
❏ Use a (1-12) or (1-20) die.

Colourful towers (AT3) Remind the children to look for duplicates. This may give rise to some interesting discussion. This activity can be applied to any number. They may choose to combine more than two numbers, such as $2 + 1 + 2 = 5$ or $1 + 3 + 1 = 5$.

Jumping frogs (AT3) The children could use practical apparatus to help them work out how to get from one lily pad to the next. Some may need explanation of the word 'subtraction'.
❏ Make the frogs do the journey in reverse.

Ribbons (AT2) Use ribbons or strips of material in a variety of lengths. The children need to have an appreciation of conservation of length and the need for accuracy when using any unit of measure. This activity can also help to improve estimation of standard measurement.

How far up the jar? (AT4) Old plastic sweet jars are ideal for the large container. Add a few drops of food colouring to the water.

Measuring strips (AT2)
❏ When the children have realised the need for using equal agreed units, they could go on to make a measuring tape using a building brick as their unit. Discuss commonly used units.

Units of measurement (AT4) The six words that the children choose will indicate the measures with which they are most familiar.
❏ Discuss imperial and metric measures.

Shape friends (AT4) If necessary use plastic or wooden shapes to help. Have a wide variety of shapes and sizes available. Some uncommon shape templates could be cut from card.

3-D structures (AT4) Encourage the children to name shapes and develop an awareness of their properties.
❏ Draw the plan or 'bird's eye' view of shapes.

The maze (AT4) Stress that instructions are given as if you are walking through the maze. A new instruction is given wherever there is a choice of direction. Enlarge it so that a stand-up figure could be made to 'walk' through it.

Finding the way (AT4)
❏ More buildings and people could be added or a larger floor grid made and objects used.

Shoes (AT5) The charts or tables could be interpreted by people not involved in the task to ensure that information is clearly presented.

Free choice (AT5)
❏ Extend the survey to other classes. What else would children like to be able to choose?

Is and is not (AT5) Offer a variety of toys.
❏ Let the children choose their own criteria.

How likely? (AT5) Some statements could fit into more than one pile, according to the children involved. The place for their own statements may be different to identical statements from other children.

Level 3

Link amounts (AT2) Children need to be familiar with the different ways of recording money - including on a calculator.

Cold days (AT2) Experience of negative numbers is necessary, at least in relation to temperature. Encourage the children to develop their own ideas on how to represent this information graphically. Offer support with labelling axes if a conventional approach is used.

Travelling by train (AT2)
❏ Draw more people in each carriage. For example, by drawing three extra people in each carriage, sets of five could be established.

Making a tables game (AT2) Remind the children that each product is only recorded once on the grid. The grid may be changed for the tables games.

The birthday party (AT2) Include the party giver as well as the guests when working out how many of each item to buy. Prices can be adjusted to the ability of the children.

Buns for bears (AT2) An extra bun has been included in the basket. The children should consider how to share one bun between four. The table helps to establish awareness of patterns and relationships. Other numbers could be used by having three or five bears.

Rolling dice (AT2) Encourage the children to work systematically. Some may need support in organising their work so that all possible solutions are explored.

Fill the jar (AT2) The size of the container and/or contents can be adjusted according to the ability of the children. A number line might help with counting the cubes (matching one to one) and to find out how close their estimate was.
❏ Find a way of grouping the cubes when counting in case they lose count (10s and 100s).

Lose or gain? (AT2) A 0-100 number line is useful. Make a selection of coins available.

Pencils (AT2)
❏ What if the box size was changed so that 6 pencils fit in each box, or 20, or 25?

PE teams (AT3)
❏ Go on to work out the numbers up to 100 that could be divided by two or five or ten.

Looking for patterns (AT3) This activity encourages children to explore number sequences and their relationships. A 0-100

number line is useful. Some children may need reminding that the pattern must be regular.

Programmed (AT3) Once the children have grasped the skill of programming the calculator, a variety of patterns can be explored.

Mr Mystery Maker (AT3) Encourage the children to be adventurous. Their 'spells' may involve more than one operation, eg double the original number, then add five.

The digital clock (AT2) There are deliberately more analogue clock faces than possible times.
❏ The children could go on to investigate which selection of four numerals would give them the greatest number of possible times.

Boxes (AT2) Make a selection of different-sized boxes available. It is important that the children have had some previous experience of finding volume in this way. Encourage them to calculate by putting in base layer and height or even length, width and height.

What could you use? (AT2) This activity helps children to consider what are appropriate measuring devices. Include rigid and flexible measuring tools marked with a variety of units. Introduce a trundle wheel if they have not used one before.

Guess the weight (AT2)
❏ Estimate and check the weights of much heavier or much lighter objects. Which do the children find harder to do?

Shape sorting (AT4)
There are many ways in which the children might choose to sort the shapes. They could label the shapes, in order to record their sorting.
❏ If paper or card is used to make the shapes, keep the off-cuts as part of the set.

Cut and sort (AT4)
❏ Draw five lines across an A4 sheet in a different way to the example given. The lines must always go from one edge to another.

Buried treasure (AT4) It might help to draw the treasure on pieces of paper that fit the grid.

Structures with cubes (AT4) The children need to understand the term 'plane of symmetry.'

Cinema visit (AT5) This activity may act as a stimulus for other time-planning exercises.

Favourite day (AT5) The children could find other ways to present the same information. Are other ways easier or harder to understand?
❏ Extend the survey to all classes. Are the results the same if adults and children are surveyed separately? If not, why not?

Colours (AT5) Either colour a blank die or use sticky spots to colour a manufactured die.

Level 4

Chocolate pieces (AT2) Practical experience of common fractions is necessary. This activity is intended to reinforce understanding by showing that an object can be divided into equal parts without each part being identical in shape.

Bigger and bigger (AT2) A calculator will help. No decimals are involved, but children who are confident using them should do so when making up their own missing numbers tables.

New uniforms (AT2) Start by making simple symmetrical designs, then more creative ones with the colours more spread out.

Which number? (AT2) This could be a co-operative activity. It will reinforce the idea that tables do not stop at 10x10. The children should find a suitable way of recording their findings.

Possible products (AT2) Sorting and classifying results is an important part of this activity. Pupils may need some support in devising a system to ensure that all possible results are obtained.

Stock check (AT2)
❏ Write an order so that all items are in stock for the next three weeks, based on the sales figures given as being the average for any week.

Can you calculate? (AT2) The idea of this sheet is not to carry out each calculation exactly but to quickly look for an approximate answer. Encourage the children to make up their own questions and answers. What helps them to find the correct answer quickly? What confuses them?

Sharing the bill (AT2) If using a calculator, the children will need to be able to read a display to the nearest whole number.
❑ Work out how much service charge is paid on each bill from Greens Fish Restaurant.

Matching the pairs (AT3)
❑ The children could explore equivalencies using other operations, or a mixture of operations. They could also explore fractions that are equivalent. A calculator may be helpful.

Square numbers (AT3) The aim of this activity is to encourage children to look for relationships in numbers and means of expressing them. This links with 'Triangles and squares' (page 111).

Starting numbers (AT3) The children will have to employ different strategies and mental calculations to ensure their puzzles work out.

Mystery picture (AT3) Remind the children to read the x co-ordinate before the y co-ordinate.

Plotting shapes (AT3)
❑ Ask the children to plot their own shapes and try doubling them. This may lead to using co-ordinates in other quadrants.

Gold blocks (AT4) If 1cm cubes are not available, other cubes could be used and the number adjusted accordingly.

Plasticine weights (AT2) Allow the children to make more than one of some weights.

Cubes and cuboids (AT4) Children need to be familiar with handling cubes to find volume.
❑ Ask each child to make three or four cubes and cuboids. Write the dimensions for each on a piece of card. Play a matching game.

How much time? (AT2) This activity could be done in pairs. Is it easier to estimate when doing or watching the activity?

Angles and lines (AT4) Equipment such as geostrips or straws and pipe cleaners might help the children to investigate shapes.

Pyramid (AT4)
❑ Make a collection of pyramids and explore ways of making new shapes with them.

Rotating shapes (AT4) Use rotation and reflection as ways of fitting on the shapes.

Logo designs (AT4) Previous experience of Logo and writing simple programs is necessary. Let the children test and adjust their predictions.

Rotation (AT4) Use tracing paper or several templates to check the suggestions.

Happy birthday (AT5) The children should use the mean average for this activity but discussion of mode and median averages could follow.

Snacks (AT5) The children should try out some questions before they create their diagram.
❑ How does the task change if the items are very similar or very different?

Watching television (AT5) The children should gather information and construct a frequency graph. They should look for other notable points that emerge from their study and suggest possible reasons for these results.

Totals (AT5) If a (7-12) die is not available a (1-6) die could be adapted by covering each face with a sticky spot or piece of masking tape.
❑ Investigate all the possible ways for making each total, not just the one scored most often.

Level 5

Drawing to scale (AT2) This activity makes the children consider the scale of the objects.

Powers (AT2) A calculator could be useful here. Let the children make their own version of this activity. They could collect examples of index

notation in other contexts and consider why it is used.

Use your head (AT2) By writing down and sharing their working out, the children may see that there is more than one method of arriving at a correct answer.

Make it big (AT2) The number of digits used could be limited or increased depending on the children's ability. An important part of this activity is asking them to explain or generalise about their discoveries.

Next door neighbours (AT2) The children will find a need to record their working out. Ensure that they know the term 'consecutive numbers'.

How close can you get? (AT2) This activity encourages children to handle numbers to several decimal places and to make judgements about their closeness. They should keep a record of each attempt to compare nearness to 100.

Triangles and squares (AT3) Encourage the children to express their findings in a rule or simple formula.

Find the formula (AT3) Previous experience of finding the volume of cubes and cuboids is necessary. Make available a variety of boxes and centicubes. This activity links well with 'Soap powder packets' (page 130).

Plotting (AT3) This activity gives practice in using all four quadrants. The children should also plot designs from others' co-ordinates and list the co-ordinates for others' designs.

Co-ordinates (AT3)
❑ Draw a random shape which would be less easy to guess.

Openings (AT4) Encourage the children to notice that some measurement of angle relates to opening and some relates to turning.

Packaging (AT2) Include some containers that would have been large and light or small and heavy. Also include containers that are visually deceptive such as some shampoo bottles.

Snail trace (AT4) The children need to be able to use a protractor for this activity. Tracing paper is useful for checking each other's results.

Flooring (AT2) Squared paper and a calculator may help for this activity.
❏ The children could make a design to meet a set budget, or, where figures are given, for a set area to be covered by each colour.

Congruent shapes (AT4) If children have problems identifying the congruent shapes they could trace the shapes and then move the tracings about. They could go on to identify similar shapes as well as congruent shapes.

Tourist (AT4)
❏ Go on to consider planning routes to visit tourist attractions in an area that they know.

Stop the waste (AT5) The children will have to think carefully about how to design their observation sheet. It may be best to take a small sample to start with so that adjustments to the sheet can be made if necessary.

Television times (AT5) The children will soon realise that sorting the programmes may not be easy, due to the compilation programmes.
❏ The children should suggest reasons for their findings and appreciate the influence of events such as a general election or a war.

Recipes (AT5) The conversion figures given are approximate to the nearest gram.
❏ Investigate liquid measures.

Favourites (AT5) If there are 'n' objects in a bag the probability of picking any one of these is 1/n. This activity links well with the one on page 144.

Level 6

Decimal numbers (AT2) If it is not possible to make the two piles equal, then the children should try to make them as close as possible.

Jolly jumpers (AT2) This helps children to realise that the sale item with the greatest reduction may not be the cheapest.

Sam's Bistro (AT2) Before changing the VAT, point out that prices already include VAT at 15%.
❏ Share the cost of a meal between several people. See 'Sharing the bill' (page 86).

Decimal fun! (AT2) This activity develops an appreciation of what happens when decimal numbers are divided. Depending on ability, it might be best to use multiplication only at first.

Sequences (AT3) The children should be encouraged to express their finding in a general rule or simple formula. When generating their own sequences they may find that the set of numbers given can satisfy more than one rule.

Soap powder packets (AT3) Use interlocking cubes to model different possible arrangements for the packing boxes.

Production costs (AT3) Support may be needed in understanding the concepts involved. Work in pairs or small groups. Follow up by contacting a local company to see a real-life example.

Train journeys (AT2) Use atlases to work out distances between cities.
❏ Use train timetables to explore other journey times and speeds. Investigate how average speeds are calculated.

Value for money (AT2)
❏ If an individual portion is 200 grams, work out how much it would cost to feed 50 people using (a) the smallest tin, (b) the largest tin.

Tessellating shapes (AT4) Remind the children that the shapes have to be used individually.

Tessellations (AT4) For ease of use, photocopy this activity sheet onto thin card.

Robot (AT4)
❏ If triangular dot lattice paper is not available what would the children need to draw to ensure that the model could be copied exactly?

Designer tiles (AT4) An understanding of the relationship between length of sides and area is necessary.
❏ Encourage children to generate their own designs and enlarge or reduce as required.

Mini-man and Maxi-man (AT4) The word 'size' is used so that children can interpret it in a number of ways, eg height, width, area.

Measuring heights (AT4) Previous practical experience of using sighting triangles to work out height is necessary.
❏ Make a scale drawing of the objects that have been measured.

Guest speaker (AT5) The children should think of what questions they need to ask and how to ask them, what they need to record and how to do it.
❏ A similar survey could be carried out for favourite television programmes.

Spoilt for choice! (AT5) The most valuable aspect of this exercise is actually carrying out the survey. The children will see how effective their data collection sheet is and where adjustments or alterations could be made.

Throwing (AT5) If this activity is impractical to test, it could be adapted, eg 'Do people with longer fingers have larger writing?', 'Do people with larger feet take longer paces?'

Twins (AT5) The children might choose to work this out as a list or as a two-way entry table. Which way makes it easier for them to check that they have got all the possibilities?

What are the chances? (AT5) The children will need to have an understanding of certain number properties and be able to say, for example, how many prime numbers are in the range from 1 to 100.
❏ By taking all of the square numbers out, what are the chances of picking out an odd number? An even triangular number?

Level	Page	Name of activity	AT2	AT3	AT4	AT5
1	11	Sets	✓		✓	
	12	Bags of apples	✓		✓	
	13	Dominoes	✓		✓	
	14	Sweet boxes	✓		✓	
	15	Lollipops	✓			
	16	Pattern repeats		✓		
	17	Flowers		✓		
	18	Heaviest/lightest			✓	
	19	Classroom shop	✓		✓	
	20	Morning routine			✓	
	21	True or false?			✓	
	22	Snakes			✓	
	23	Make a pattern			✓	
	24	Shapes with cubes				✓
	25	How many sides?				✓
	26	Where?				✓
	27	Piles				✓
	28	Toys for sorting				
	29	Belongings				
	30	What might happen?				
2	31	Halves	✓			
	32	Three-digit numbers	✓			
	33	Number cards	✓			
	34	Difference pairs	✓			
	35	Money track	✓			
	36	Guessing handfuls	✓			
	37	How many?	✓			
	38	Look-out towers		✓		
	39	Making 10		✓		
	40	Colourful towers		✓		
	41	Jumping frogs		✓		
	42	Ribbons	✓			
	43	How far up the jar?	✓		✓	
	44	Measuring strips	✓			

Level	Page	Name of activity	AT2	AT3	AT4	AT5
2	45	Units of measurement			✓	
	46	Shape friends			✓	✓
	47	3-D structures			✓	✓
	48	The maze			✓	✓
	49	Finding the way				✓
	50	Shoes				
	51	Free choice				
	52	Is and is not				
	53	How likely?				
3	54	Link amounts	✓			
	55	Cold days	✓			
	56	Travelling by train	✓			
	57	Making a tables game	✓			
	58	The birthday party	✓			
	59	Buns for bears	✓			
	60	Rolling dice	✓			
	61	Fill the jar	✓			
	62	Lose or gain?		✓		
	63	Pencils		✓		
	64	PE teams		✓		
	65	Looking for patterns	✓	✓		
	66	Programmed	✓			
	67	Mr Mystery Maker	✓			
	68	The digital clock	✓			
	69	Boxes				
	70	What could you use?				
	71	Guess the weight				
	72	Shape sorting			✓	
	73	Cut and sort			✓	
	74	Buried treasure			✓	
	75	Structures with cubes			✓	
	76	Cinema visit				✓
	77	Favourite day				✓
	78	Colours				✓

Level	Page	Name of activity	AT2	AT3	AT4	AT5
4	79	Chocolate pieces	✓			
	80	Bigger and bigger	✓			
	81	New uniforms	✓			
	82	Which number?	✓			
	83	Possible products	✓			
	84	Stock check	✓			
	85	Can you calculate?	✓			
	86	Sharing the bill	✓			
	87	Matching the pairs		✓		
	88	Square numbers		✓		
	89	Starting numbers		✓		
	90	Mystery picture	✓	✓		
	91	Plotting shapes	✓	✓		
	92	Gold blocks		✓		
	93	Plasticine weights			✓	
	94	Cubes and cuboids			✓	
	95	How much time?			✓	
	96	Angles and lines			✓	
	97	Pyramid			✓	
	98	Rotating shapes			✓	
	99	Logo designs			✓	
	100	Rotation			✓	
	101	Happy birthday				✓
	102	Snacks				✓
	103	Watching television				✓
	104	Totals				✓
5	105	Drawing to scale	✓			✓
	106	Powers	✓			✓
	107	Use your head	✓			✓
	108	Make it big	✓			✓
	109	Next door neighbours	✓			
	110	How close can you get?	✓			
	111	Triangles and squares		✓	✓	

Level	Page	Name of activity	AT2	AT3	AT4	AT5
5	112	Find the formula		✓		
	113	Plotting		✓		
	114	Co-ordinates		✓		
	115	Openings	✓			
	116	Packaging	✓			
	117	Snail trace				
	118	Flooring			✓	
	119	Congruent shapes			✓	
	120	Tourist				✓
	121	Stop the waste				✓
	122	Television times				✓
	123	Recipes				✓
	124	Favourites				
6	125	Decimal numbers	✓			
	126	Jolly jumpers	✓			
	127	Sam's Bistro	✓			
	128	Decimal fun!	✓			
	129	Sequences	✓			
	130	Soap powder packets		✓		
	131	Production costs		✓		
	132	Train journeys		✓		
	133	Value for money			✓	
	134	Tessellating shapes			✓	
	135	Tessellations			✓	
	136	Robot			✓	
	137	Designer tiles			✓	
	138	Mini-man and Maxi-man				
	139	Measuring heights				
	140	Guest speaker				✓
	141	Spoilt for choice!				✓
	142	Throwing				✓
	143	Twins				✓
	144	What are the chances?				✓

Sets

♣ Cut out the sets. Count how many things there are in each set.

♣ Stick them in your book, starting with a set of one and ending with a set of ten.

♣ Write the number of things in each set.

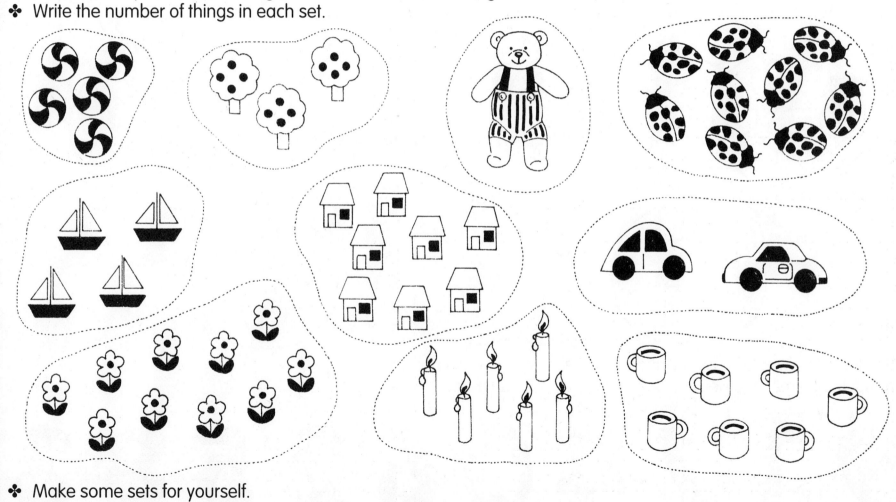

♣ Make some sets for yourself.

Bags of apples

 # Bags of apples

♣ Count how many apples in each bag. Put the correct number on each label.

♣ Cut out the numbers below and put them in order, from smallest to largest.
♣ Put the correct number of buttons or cubes with each one.

9 1 7 4 0 6 2 5 8 3

Name _____

Dominoes

❖ Look at a set of dominoes. Find a domino which has 8 spots on it altogether.

❖ Find all the dominoes which have a total of 8 spots on them. Draw these dominoes here.

❖ Make these dominoes have a total of 6 spots. Each one should be different.

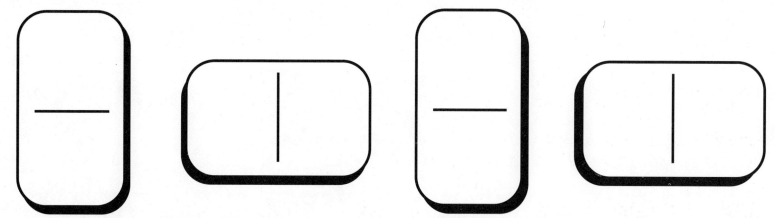

❖ Can you find any dominoes in the set like the ones you have made?

❖ Are there any that are different to the ones that you have made?

Sweet boxes

Sweet boxes

♣ Cut out these boxes of sweets. Put together the boxes that make 10. How many sets of 10 can you make?

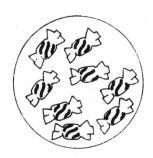

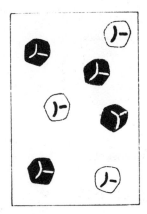
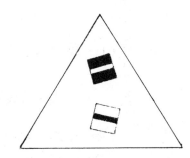

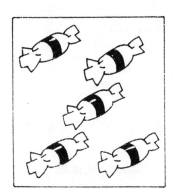

Mathematics

Lollipops

✿ Guess how many lollipops there are.

✿ Now count them. How many are there?

✿ If you gave some children one lollipop each, how many children would have lollipops?

✿ Now colour each lollipop.

✿ How many lollipops have red on them?

♣ How many lollipops have green on them?

✿ How many lollipops have blue on them?

Name _____

♣ Continue the patterns.

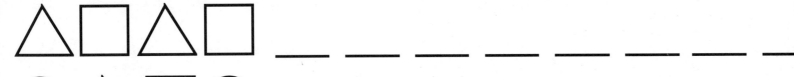

- -

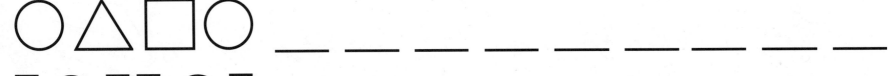

- -

- -

♣ Use some or all of these shapes to make your own repeating pattern.

- -

♣ Use some or all of these shapes to make your own repeating pattern.

- -

Mathematics

Name _____

Flowers

❧ Draw the next four flowers in this pattern. Colour them in.

❧ Make two different flower patterns of your own.

Name _____

Heaviest/lightest

Heaviest / lightest

❖ Find these objects.

ball of Plasticine   bean bag   stone

❖ Put them in order of weight, lightest to heaviest. Draw them in the boxes below.

Heaviest

Lightest

❖ Choose another object. Weigh it. Where does it go in the order? Draw them all in the boxes below.

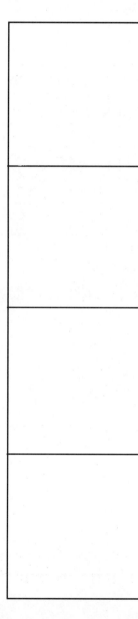

Heaviest

Lightest

Mathematics

Classroom shop

❖ Here are some of the things in the class shop.

❖ Use 1p coins. Give each of the children below 10p. Will each child have enough money to buy all of the things on their list?

SHOPPING LIST

apple   2p

choc ice   5p

chocolate   3p
bar

Reshina

SHOPPING LIST

cake   6p

apple   2p

choc ice 5p

Sally

SHOPPING LIST

crisps   7p

lollipop   2p

biscuit   1p

Leon

❖ Put prices on these shopping lists.
Then work out how much each bill will be.

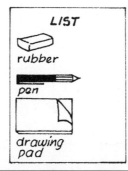

LIST

rubber

pan

drawing
pad

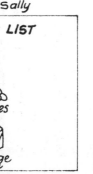

LIST

nuts

grapes

orange
juice

LIST

comic

choc ice

crisps

LIST

pear

biscuits

cake

Morning routine

Here are some pictures of things you might do in the morning. Think about the order in which you do them.

❖ Draw them in the boxes below in the order that you do them.

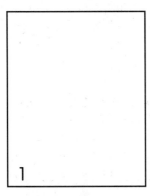 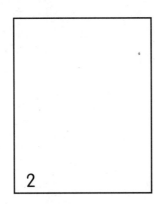 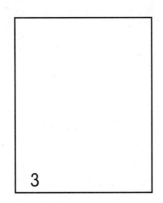 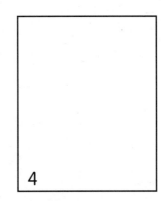

1   2   3   4   5

❖ Draw some pictures, in order, of what you do after school.

Name _____

True or false?

♣ Use a balance and the objects to prove whether the following are true or false. Colour in the correct box.

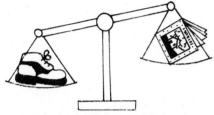

A shoe is heavier than a reading book.

True	False

A ruler is heavier than a pair of scissors.

True	False

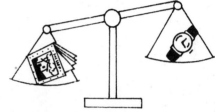

A reading book is heavier than a watch.

True	False

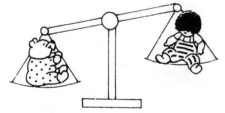

A doll is lighter than a teddy.

True	False

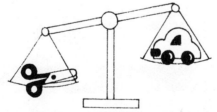

A toy car is lighter than a pair of scissors.

True	False

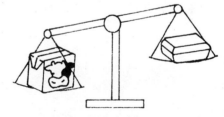

A margarine tub is lighter than a milk carton.

True	False

♣ Draw some true or false balances to try on your friends.

- ❧ Cut out the snakes. Put them in order, from the shortest to the longest.
- ❧ Cut out the labels and put them next to the longest and shortest snakes. Stick the snakes and labels in your book.

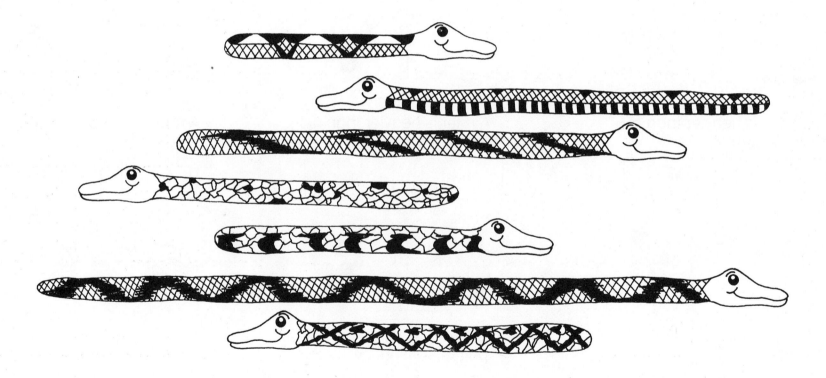

- ❧ Find something in your classroom longer than the longest snake.
- ❧ Find something in your classroom shorter than the shortest snake.

longest	shortest

Name _____

Make a Pattern

❖ This is a pattern made from squares, oblongs and triangles.

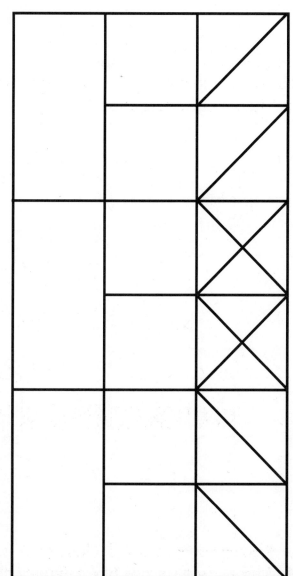

❖ Colour the pattern.

❖ Colour the shapes below. Cut along the lines. Use the shapes to make a pattern of your own.

Name _____

Shapes with cubes

 Shapes with cubes

❖ Look carefully at the shapes below. Each shape is made with 5 interlocking cubes. Try to make each one. Can you make other shapes with 5 cubes that are not shown here?

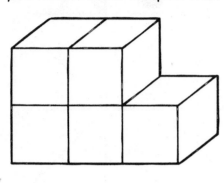

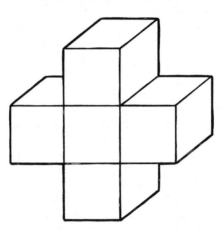

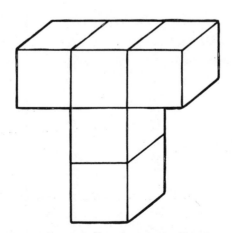

❖ Draw one shape you have made here.

❖ Make some shapes of your own with 6 cubes in each shape.

Name _____

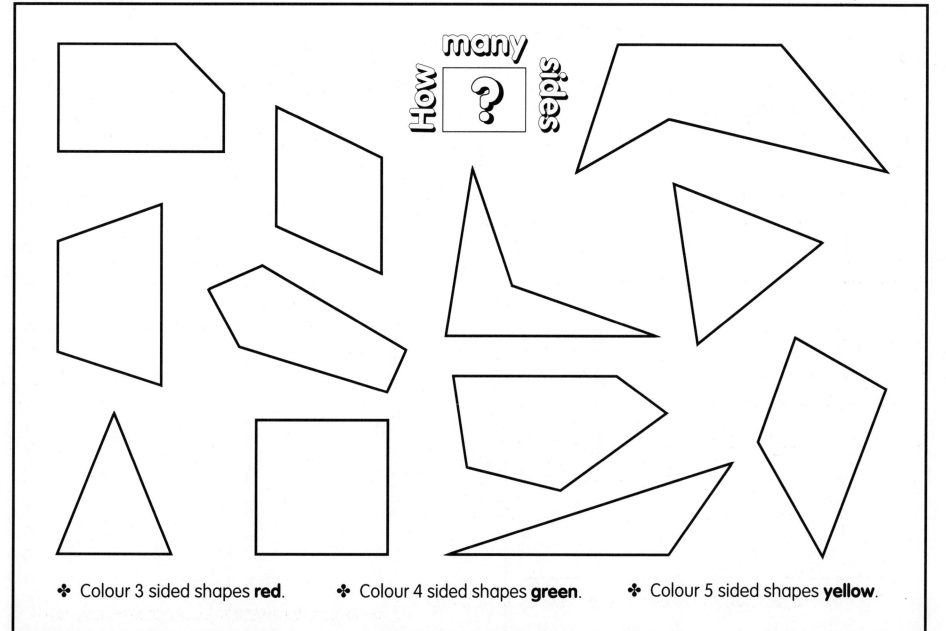

❖ Colour 3 sided shapes **red**.   ❖ Colour 4 sided shapes **green**.   ❖ Colour 5 sided shapes **yellow**.

Where?

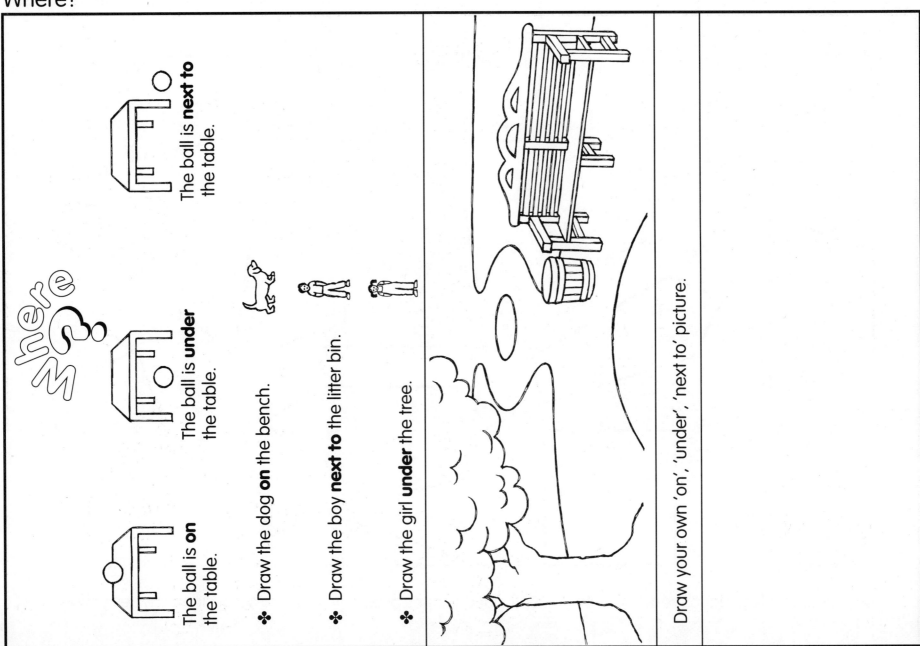

The ball is **on** the table.

The ball is **under** the table.

The ball is **next to** the table.

✤ Draw the dog **on** the bench.

✤ Draw the boy **next to** the litter bin.

✤ Draw the girl **under** the tree.

Draw your own 'on', 'under', 'next to' picture.

Name _____

Piles

♣ Cut around the pictures. Sort the pictures into piles of things that you think belong together.

♣ Why do you think that they belong together? Could you sort them in a different way?

Toys for sorting

✤ Colour the toys and then cut them out. Can you sort these toys?
How many different ways can you sort them?

✤ Choose 6 toys from the toy box. Draw a picture of each on a separate sheet of paper.
Think about different ways of sorting your pictures.

Name _____

Belongings

♣ Draw lines linking the owners to their belongings.

DOG FOOD

Name _____

What might happen?

What might happen?

❖ What could happen next? Cut out the pictures below and sort them to go with the pictures above.

❖ Draw your own set of pictures of what might happen when you get up in the morning.

Mathematics

Halves

❖ Make tracings of the shapes below and keep them safely on one side.

❖ Cut out the shapes on this paper. Cut each shape in half. Colour each half a different colour.

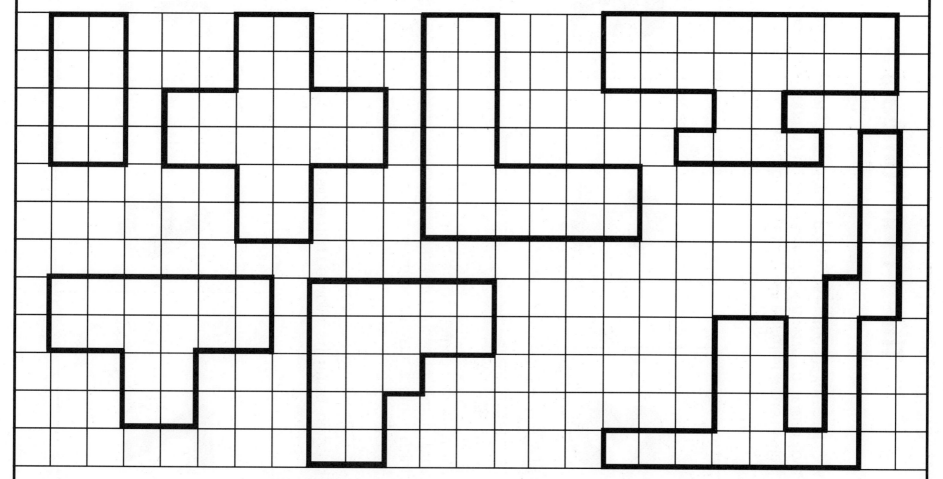

❖ When you have cut and coloured each shape, fit them back onto your traced shapes.

Name _____

Three-digit numbers

Three-digit numbers

♣ What three-digit numbers can you make using these numerals? You may only use each numeral once in each number. Write the numbers in order from the smallest to the largest.

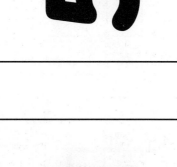

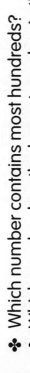

♣ Which number contains most hundreds?
♣ Which number has the largest number in the tens column?
♣ Which number has the largest number in the units column?

♣ Try again, using the following numerals.

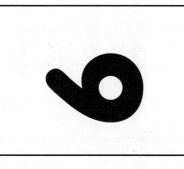

Mathematics

Name _____

✣ Cut out the number cards and put them in order from the lowest to the highest.

✣ Write any number from 0 to 99 on the blank cards and put them into the correct place in the lowest to highest order.

✣ On the back of each card, draw an abacus picture to match the number. One has been done for you.

Can you think of a game to play with a friend, using these cards?

89	45	57
23	94	69
17	38	70

Name _____

Difference pairs

9 6 3 **Difference pairs** 4 0 12

✤ The difference between 3 and 7 is 4.
✤ Find the pairs of numbers where the difference between them is 4. Join the pair together by drawing a line.

✤ You could use the number tracks below to help you. To check that the difference between 3 and 7 is 4, put 3 buttons or counters on one number line and 7 buttons or counters on the other. Count that the difference between them is 4.

1	2	3	4	5	6	7	8	9	10	11	12	13	14
1	2	3	4	5	6	7	8	9	10	11	12	13	14

✤ Write some more pairs of numbers where the difference between them is 4.

Name _____

Money track

START
2p 1p 1p  2p 2p

2p

1p

1p

2p

2p

1p

> ✤ You need: 10 (1p) coins, 11 (2p) coins, a die and
> a sand-timer.
> ✤ Place the coins on the track as shown. Set the sand-timer.
> ✤ Start at START.
> ✤ Throw the die. Count on that number around the track.
> Pick up the coin that you land on. Keep going around until
> the sand-timer runs out. How much have you collected?
> ✤ Put the coins back on the track. Have another try. Do you
> think you will collect more, less or the same amount this time?

1p 2p 1p 1p 2p 2p 1p 2p

Name _____

Guessing handfuls

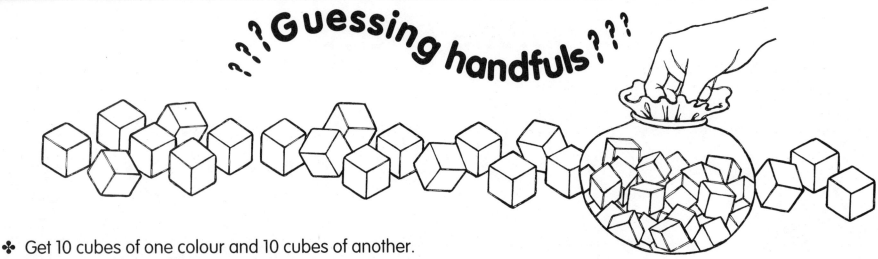

✣ Get 10 cubes of one colour and 10 cubes of another.
✣ Put the two sets of cubes into a bag.
✣ Now put one hand into the bag and take out as many cubes as your hand will hold.
✣ Look and guess how many of each colour and how many altogether.
✣ Count them to check how good you are at guessing.
✣ Write your guesses in the box below.

Try	Colour _____	Colour _____	Altogether
1			
2			
3			
4			
5			
6			

✣ You might like to try using more cubes, fewer cubes, smaller cubes or three different colours.

How many?

♣ Take a handful of small toys out of a box. How many toys do you think you have picked up?
After you have guessed, count them to check.

♣ Take three more handfuls. Do you always pick up the same number of toys?
If not, do you pick up roughly the same number of toys?
Show your results on a bar chart.

Number of toys

5

4

3

2

1

| 1st handful | 2nd handful | 3rd handful | 4th handful |

♣ Try the activity using a box of building bricks.

♣ Try the activity using a box of fir cones.

♣ Try the activity using a box of buttons.

Look-out towers

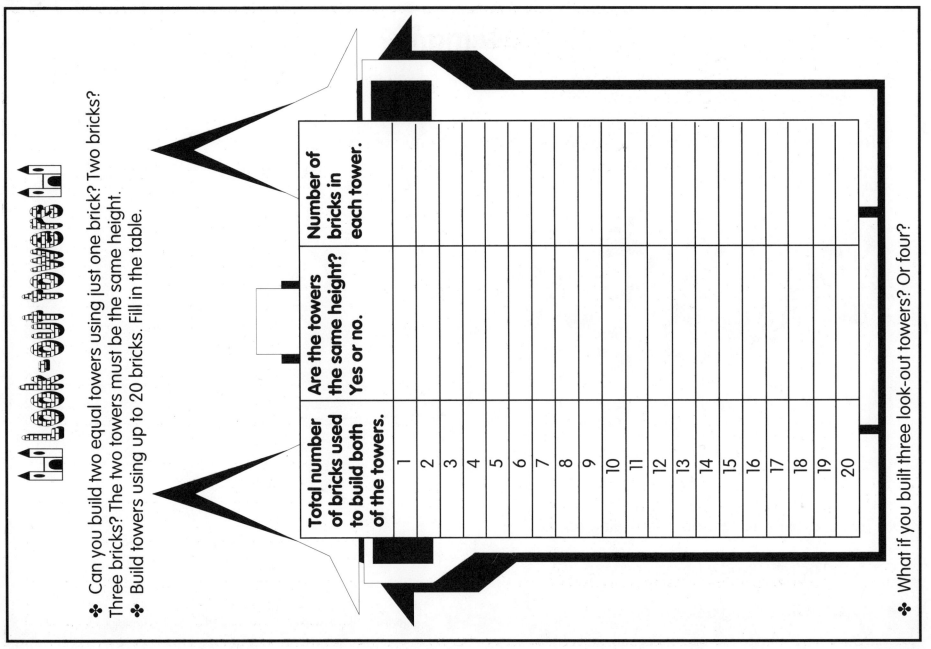

Look-out towers

✤ Can you build two equal towers using just one brick? Two bricks? Three bricks? The two towers must be the same height.
✤ Build towers using up to 20 bricks. Fill in the table.

Total number of bricks used to build both of the towers.	Are the towers the same height? Yes or no.	Number of bricks in each tower.
1		
2		
3		
4		
5		
6		
7		
8		
9		
10		
11		
12		
13		
14		
15		
16		
17		
18		
19		
20		

✤ What if you built three look-out towers? Or four?

Making 10

♣ You will need some red and blue cubes and a (0-9) or (1-10) die.

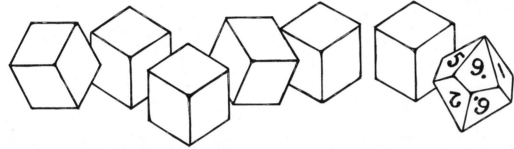

♣ Throw the die and put out that number of blue cubes. Now guess how many red cubes you will need to make 10 cubes in all. Check to see if you are right.

♣ Fill in your results on the chart.

♣ Use squared paper to show all the ways of making 10.

Blue cubes	Red cubes
10	
9	
8	
7	
6	
5	
4	
3	
2	
1	
0	

Name _____

Colourful towers

Colourful towers

✤ Choose some cubes in two different colours. You could choose green and yellow.

✤ Build towers of 5 bricks. Make each one different by arranging the colours in a different way.

✤ Draw your results on the squared paper below.

✤ Write a number sentence for each tower, for example 3+2=5.

Name _____

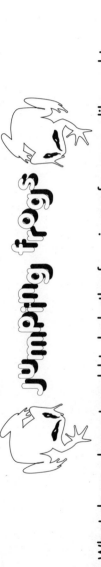

Jumping frogs

❖ What do you have to add to help the frog jump from one lily-pad to the next?

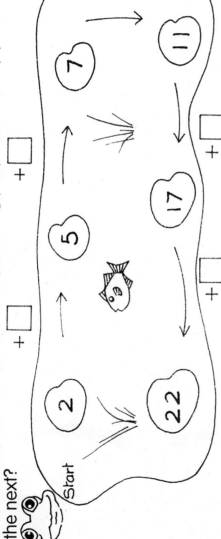

Start — 2 — 5 — 7 — 11 — 17 — 22

❖ Write down what you have done in the following way:

$2 + \square = 5$

$5 + \square = 7$

$7 + \square = 11$

$11 + \square = 17$

$17 + \square = 22$

❖ Make your own jumping frog activity.

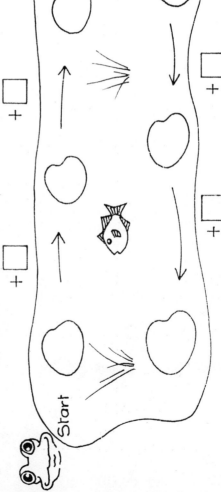

Start

$\square + \square = \square$

$\square + \square = \square$

$\square + \square = \square$

$\square + \square = \square$

$\square + \square = \square$

❖ Try the same activity using subtraction instead of addition.

Ribbons

✤ Select 5 or 6 pieces of ribbon of different lengths.
✤ Estimate how many new pencils will fit along each ribbon. Write your guess in the box below.
Then check to see how close your guess was.

Ribbon	Guess	Actual length
1		
2		
3		
4		
5		
6		

✤ If you used milk straws instead of pencils, would you need more or less of them than the number of pencils you used for each ribbon?
✤ Estimate first and then see if you were right.

Name _____

How far up the jar?

♣ Take a large, clear plastic jar and stick a strip of paper or masking tape from top to bottom so that you can write on it. Collect a selection of other containers.

♣ Take each container in turn and fill it with water. Draw a line across the strip of paper to show where you predict the water level will reach when you empty the small container into the large jar. Now pour the water into the jar to find out how close you are. Empty the jar and try again with a different container.

♣ Add a new strip of paper or masking tape to the side of the jar. Use a cup and water to make a 'cupfuls' measure. Predict and test how many cupfuls of water each of your other containers hold.

Name _____

Measuring strips

Measuring strips

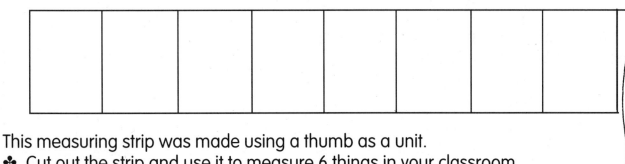

This measuring strip was made using a thumb as a unit.

❖ Cut out the strip and use it to measure 6 things in your classroom.

❖ Use your own thumb to make a measuring strip by drawing lines one thumb width apart along the strip below.
❖ Use it to measure the same 6 things.

❖ Are the results the same?
❖ If they are the same - why?
❖ If they are not the same - why not?

Name _____

Units of measurement

♣ Look at the words below. What is each unit a measurement of?
Cut out the words and stick them into the table.

metre	kilogram	kilometre	quart
minute	centimetre	pint	centilitre
mile	hour	litre	ounce
gallon	gram	pound	stone
inch	week	second	year

length	capacity	weight	time

♣ Choose 6 of the words from the table and write below something that they could be used to measure.

Unit of measurement	Possible use

Name _____

Shape friends

Shape friends

✤ These are shape friends.

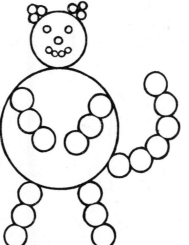

✤ Draw another shape friend. You can use just one type of shape or lots of different shapes.

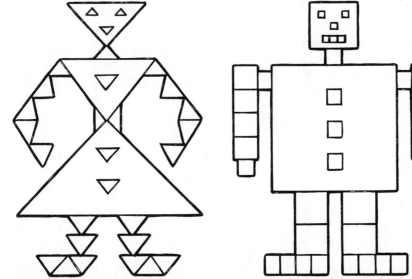

Mathematics

3-D structures

❖ Get a set of three-dimensional (3-D) shapes.
❖ Look carefully at the drawings below and find the shapes which match each one.

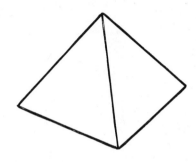 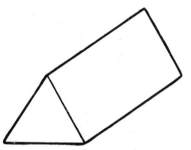 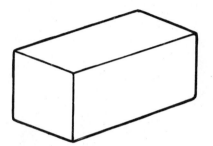 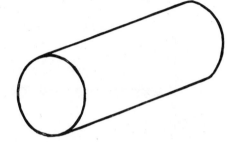

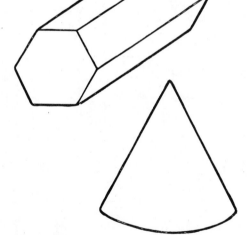

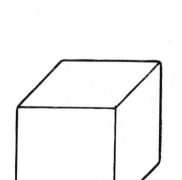

Draw your structure here.

❖ Use all of these shapes to make a structure. Try and draw what you have made.

Name _____

The maze

❖ Imagine you are walking through the maze. What do you think you will reach when you get out?

❖ Follow the instructions to get through the maze. Move forward to each junction where instructions are given for your next move.

F means move **forward**
L means turn **left**
R means turn **right**

F.R.F.L.F.R.F.R.F.L.F.F.L.F.F.R.F.R.F.L.F.

Remember to stop at each junction before following the next instruction.

❖ Write instructions below to get from the start to a different prize.

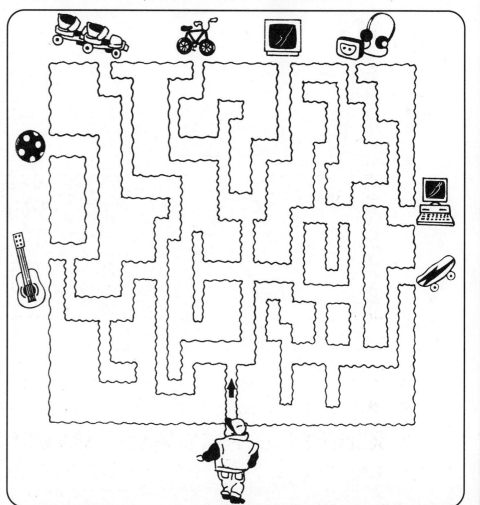

Name _____

Finding the way

✤ For Sam to get to the adventure playground he has to:

Go forward 4. Turn left at the library. Go forward 3. Turn right. Go forward 6.

✤ Write the route instructions for each child to reach the adventure playground.
✤ Draw two more children onto this street grid and write instructions for them too.

Name _____

Shoes

Shoes

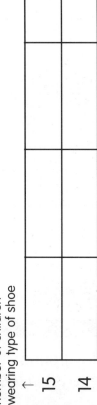

♣ Look at the shoes worn by the people in your class. Collect information about the different types of shoes you can see. How many people wear each type of shoe?

♣ Make a chart or table to show what you have found out.

→ types of shoe

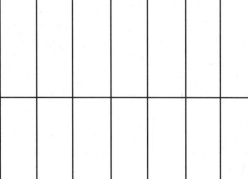
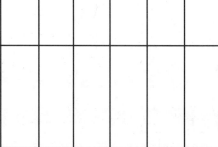
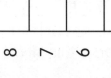

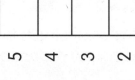
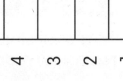

number of children
wearing type of shoe
↑ 15
14
13
12
11
10
9
8
7
6
5
4
3
2
1

Name _____

Free choice

✤ A class decided to find out what was the favourite 'free choice' activity. They carried out a survey of every child in the class. This is the way they recorded their findings.

Lego	X	X	X	X	X	X	X	X
sand	X	X	X	X				
painting	X	X	X					
train set	X	X	X	X	X			
reading	X	X	X	X	X	X		
shop	X	X	X	X	X			
jigsaw puzzles	X	X	X					

They found out that Lego was the favourite activity.
✤ What activity was the second favourite?
✤ How many children did they ask?
✤ Carry out a survey in your class to find out the most popular free-choice activity.

Is and is not

Is and is not

❖ Make a collection of toys for sorting. Include some metal toys that have wheels.
❖ Think about the different ways of sorting these toys.
❖ Look at this chart. Which toys would go into each section? Write the name of the toy or draw a picture of it in the correct part of the chart.

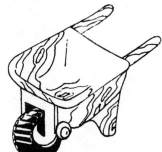

	Metal	Not metal
Wheels		
No wheels		

Name _____

How likely?

♣ Cut along the dotted lines.
♣ Sort the statements into three piles,
one pile for each category.

certain   uncertain   impossible

♣ Make up 2 more statements of your own to go into each category and write them on the blank strips.

Tomorrow I will be younger than I am today.	Tomorrow the sun will rise.
Tomorrow the sun will shine.	I will get some new clothes this month.
My old clothes will wear out.	I will be three years older by tomorrow morning.

Name _____

Link amounts

Link amounts

Each amount of money below has been shown in 3 different ways.
✣ Join each of the amounts that are the same, using different colours. The first one has been done for you.

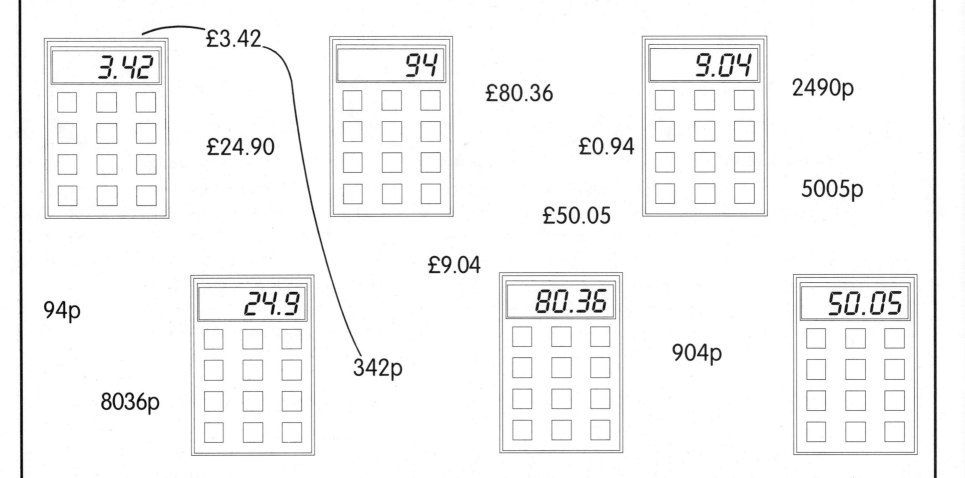

£3.42

£80.36

2490p

£24.90

£0.94

5005p

£50.05

£9.04

94p

904p

8036p

342p

✣ Set up some similar problems for other people to solve. Don't forget to put the amounts in the calculator displays.

Name _____

Cold days

Some children recorded the outside temperatures every day for a week.
Here are the results:

Monday 10th	9°C
Tuesday 11th	8°C
Wednesday12th	7°C
Thursday 13th	7°C
Friday 14th	4°C

During the following week, the weather became much colder. Some days the temperature dropped below 0° Celsius. The children noted by how much the temperature had fallen compared with the same day of the previous week.

Monday 17th	6°C less
Tuesday 18th	8°C less
Wednesday 19th	8°C less
Thursday 20th	9°C less
Friday 21st	7°C less

♣ Complete this table to show the temperature recordings for both weeks:

Day	Date	Temp	Date	Temp
Monday	10th	9°C	17th	3°C
Tuesday	11th		18th	
Wednesday	12th		19th	
Thursday	13th		20th	
Friday	14th		21st	

Draw a graph of the temperatures for both weeks.

Name _____

Travelling by train

Travelling by train

♣ How many people can you see on the train?
♣ Draw two people in each of the empty carriages.
♣ Fill in this table:

Carriages	Total number of people
1	2
2	4
3	
4	
5	

♣ How many people do you think there would be in:

Number of carriages	Guess	Check
10 carriages		
20 carriages		
50 carriages		
100 carriages		

♣ Use a calculator - but guess first!

Mathematics

Making a tables game

♣ Roll two (1 - 6) dice and multiply your scores together.
♣ Put the answer into one of the spaces on the grid below.
♣ Keep rolling the dice. Each time you get a different answer fill it in on the grid.
♣ Now think of a way of using this grid for a tables game. Write the rules on a piece of paper.
Test it on some friends.

Name _____

The birthday party

The birthday party

✤ Tom is having a birthday party.
He has invited four friends.
He has £6.50 to spend.
✤ These are the things he needs
to buy for each person:

List
paper plate
paper cup
savoury food
sweet food
drink

✣ He also needs to buy a prize for each of four games. Make a shopping list for him from the items shown.

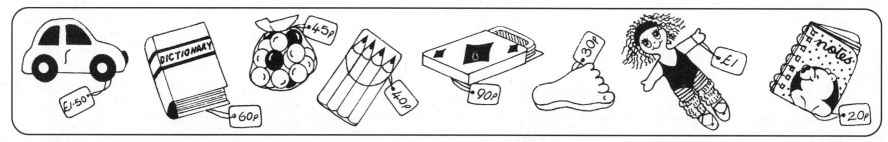

✤ If you were giving a party, what would you buy? How much would it cost?

Name _____

🐻 Buns for bears 🐻

✤ Can you share the buns in the basket so that each bear has the same number?

✤ Are there any left over?

✤ If you had 16 buns how many would each bear have?

✤ Complete this table:

If each bear is to have	I will need to buy
2 buns	8
3 buns	12
4 buns	
5 buns	
6 buns	
7 buns	
8 buns	

Rolling dice

Rolling dice

♣ Roll two (1 - 6) dice and add your scores together. What did you get?

♣ Is it possible to make all of the numbers from 0 - 12 in this way? Investigate and find out.

♣ Choose any one of the numbers below and find all the possible ways of making it by adding the scores on your two dice together.

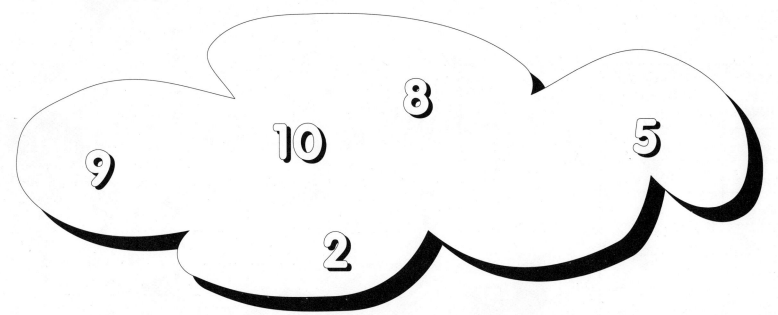

8

10

5

9

2

♣ Can you find a way of checking that you have got all of the possible solutions?

Fill the jar

✤ Fill a jar with cubes that are the same size. Estimate how many cubes are inside. Empty the jar and count the cubes.

Score ❸ if you were within 10 of the answer.
Score ❷ if you were within 20 of the answer.
Score ❶ if you were within 50 of the answer.

✤ Find cubes that are smaller or larger than the ones you used before. Fill the jar with them. Estimate the number of cubes as before. Keep your score.
✤ Try the same activity with different containers.

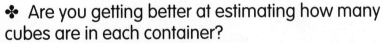
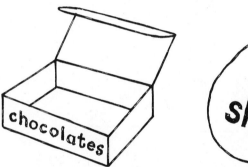

✤ Are you getting better at estimating how many cubes are in each container?
✤ You could try filling the containers with other things, such as beads or peas.
✤ Ask your friends to try this activity. Do any of them score more than you?

Container	Estimate	Correct number	Difference	Score
Jar				

Name _____

Lose or gain?

Lose or gain?

❖ The Post Office only had 10p coins in the till. The cashier decided that the fairest way to cash postal orders would be to give each person their amount to the nearest 10p. So Leah will receive 40p. What will the others receive?

Leah | 36p | gets | 40p

Hannah | 12p | gets | [ ]

Janine | 91p | gets | [ ]

David | 49p | gets | [ ]

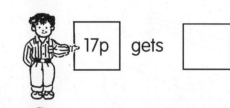

Abdul | 17p | gets | [ ]

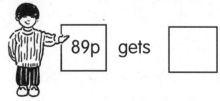

Chi | 89p | gets | [ ]

❖ Who will gain the most?

❖ Suppose the Post Office only had 5p coins in its till and paid each customer to the nearest 5p. Write down what each person would get.

Mathematics

Name _____

Pencils

♣ At the factory, pencils are packed in boxes. 10 pencils go in each box.

♣ How many boxes can be filled with 72 pencils? Are there any pencils left over? Fill in the table:

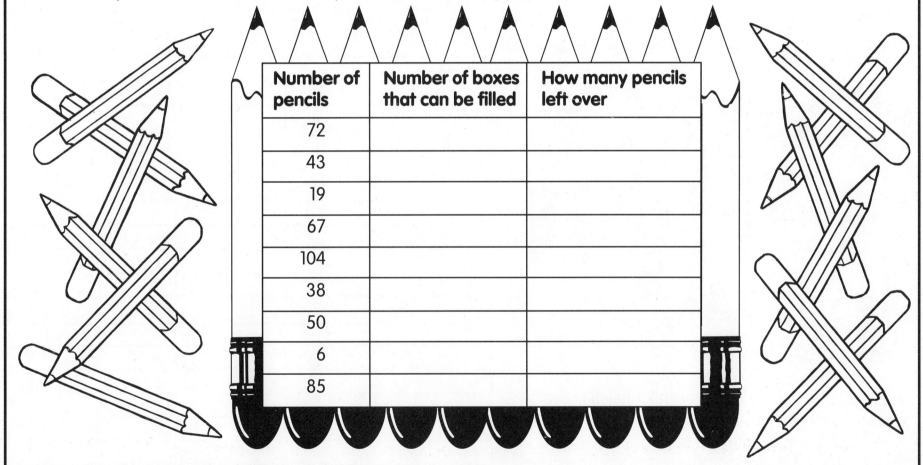

Number of pencils	Number of boxes that can be filled	How many pencils left over
72		
43		
19		
67		
104		
38		
50		
6		
85		

♣ How many pencils would exactly fill 3 boxes? 15 boxes? 7 boxes?

Name _____

PE teams

There are thirty children in the class. They need to split up into teams for different games in their PE lessons. Sometimes children are away, so the class is smaller.

❖ Decide for each number of children left in the class whether they could split into teams of 2, 5 or 10 without anyone being left out.
❖ Fill in the table, saying how many teams can be made. One has been done for you.

Number of children in class	Can make teams of 2 exactly	Can make teams of 5 exactly	Can make teams of 10 exactly
10	5	2	1
11			
12			
13			
14			
15			
16			
17			
18			
19			
20			
21			
22			
23			
24			
25			
26			
27			
28			
29			
30			

Name _____

Looking for patterns

❖ Look carefully at the number sequences below. Write in the next 3 numbers for each.
❖ Write a sentence for each pattern to explain what is happening.

❖ Make up some number sequences for other children to try.

Programmed

Programmed

✤ These calculators have been programmed so that each time you put in a number and press [=] a certain output is given. Can you work out what is happening?

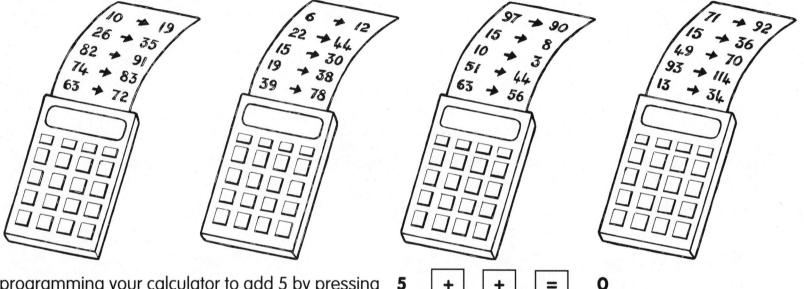

10 → 19	6 → 12	97 → 90	71 → 92
26 → 35	22 → 44	15 → 8	15 → 36
82 → 91	15 → 30	10 → 3	49 → 70
74 → 83	19 → 38	51 → 44	93 → 114
63 → 72	39 → 78	63 → 56	13 → 34

✤ Try programming your calculator to add 5 by pressing **5** [**+**] [**+**] [**=**] **0**

✤ Then put in any number and press the [**=**] button.

✤ Do not press [**clear**] or **0**

✤ Try changing it to add on a different number. Can you make it subtract a number?

Name _____

Mr Mystery Maker, the magician, has cast a spell on some numbers. Can you find out what he has done to them?

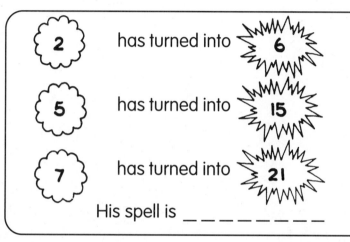

2 has turned into 6

5 has turned into 15

7 has turned into 21

His spell is _ _ _ _ _ _ _ _

✤ What spell has he cast on these numbers?

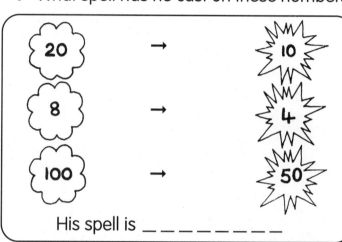

20 → 10

8 → 4

100 → 50

His spell is _ _ _ _ _ _ _ _

✤ What spell has he cast on these numbers?

10 → 21

7 → 18

1 → 12

His spell is _ _ _ _ _ _ _ _

✤ Cast some spells of your own.

The spell is _ _ _ _ _ _ _ _ _ _ _ _ _ _ _ _

The spell is _ _ _ _ _ _ _ _ _ _ _ _ _ _ _ _

Mathematics

Name _____

The digital clock

❖ If your twenty-four hour, digital clock was showing the numerals (2 0 1 6) in any order, write down all the digital times there could be.

❖ Draw the same times on the analogue clock faces below.

❖ Did you use all the clock faces?

Mathematics

Boxes

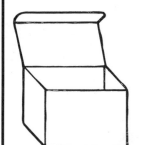
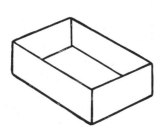

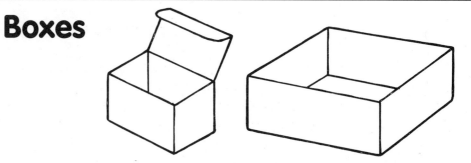

♣ Choose 3 boxes of different sizes and some cubes.

♣ Estimate how many of the cubes you think each box will hold. Write your estimate in the table. Now count them and write in the actual number.

♣ Can you find a way of working out how many cubes are required without having to completely fill the box each time?

♣ Would you need more or fewer cubes if you used larger cubes?

♣ What if the cubes were smaller?

♣ What if you have different sized cubes?

♣ Choose some different boxes and try these activities again.

Boxes	Volume	
	Estimate	**Actual**

Name _____

What could you use?

What could you use?

❖ Collect different instruments which you could use to measure length. Draw them below.

❖ Use some or all of them to help you fill in this table.

What to measure	Answer	Instrument used to measure with and reason for choosing it
The perimeter of the school playground.		
The length of the school hall.		
The height of your table.		
The width of your reading book.		
Your height.		
Your waist.		

❖ Could you have used more suitable equipment? If so, what?

❖ Ask a friend if they would have chosen to use the same equipment as you for each measurement you made. If not, why not?

Guess the weight

❖ Which do you think weighs more - a shoe or a jumper?
❖ Get one of each and estimate their weight in grams.
❖ Fill in your estimates on the chart below. Now check your estimates.
❖ Try estimating the weight of some more pairs of objects and then check your estimates. Fill in the tables.

Object	Estimated weight	Weight in grams	Object	Estimated weight	Weight in grams
shoe			jumper		
ruler			scissors		
mug			plate		
spoon			fork		
book			dictionary		

❖ Choose 3 more pairs of objects, estimate and then check their weight.

Object	Estimated weight	Weight in grams	Object	Estimated weight	Weight in grams

❖ Does a shoe always weigh more than a jumper or a jumper always weigh more than a shoe? Test your theory.

Shape sorting

Name _____

Shape sorting

♣ Cut along the dotted lines. Which shapes do you think are the same in some way. Why?
♣ Find at least three different ways to sort the shapes. Record what you have done.
♣ Make some shapes of your own to sort.

Name _____

Cut and sort

♣ Cut along the dotted lines and sort the shapes according to the number of sides of each.
♣ Think of other ways of sorting these shapes.

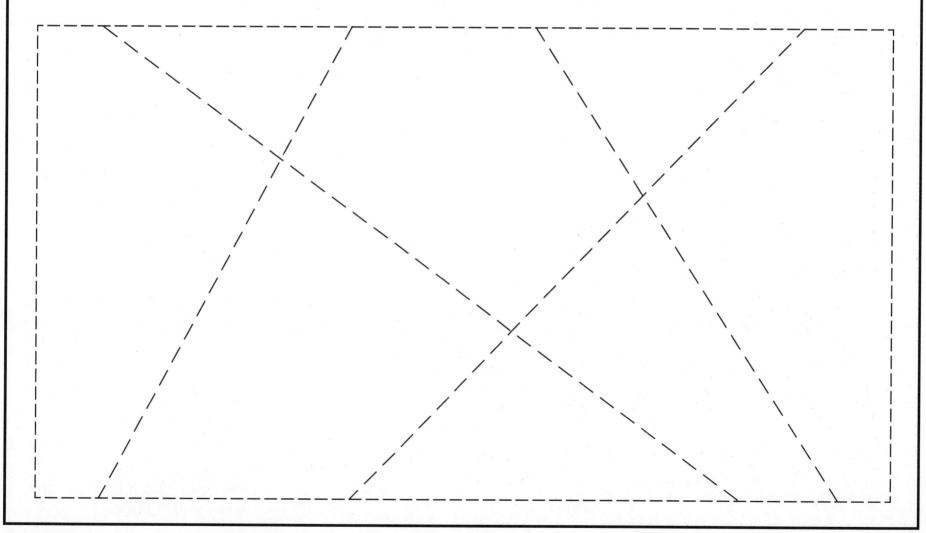

Name _____

Buried treasure

Buried treasure

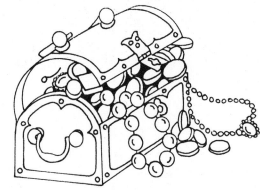

The ring is buried north of the treasure chest.

The necklace is buried south of the treasure chest.

The sword is buried west of the treasure chest.

The shield is buried east of the treasure chest.

The bracelet is buried south-east of the treasure chest.

The gold coins are buried south-west of the treasure chest.

The crown is buried north-west of the treasure chest.

The gold bar is buried north-east of the treasure chest.

❖ By following these directions, draw the treasures around the treasure chest on the chart.

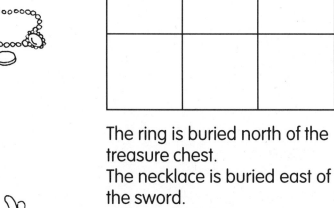

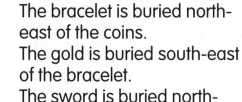

The ring is buried north of the treasure chest.
The necklace is buried east of the sword.
The bracelet is buried north-east of the coins.
The gold is buried south-east of the bracelet.
The sword is buried north-west of the shield.
The treasure chest is buried north-west of the crown.

❖ Find the treasure and the treasure chest and draw them in the correct spaces on the blank chart above.

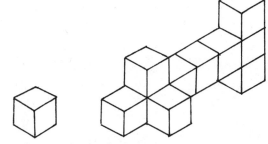

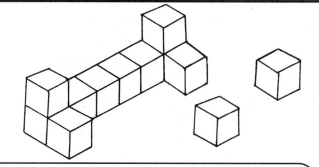

✤ Using interlocking cubes, make different structures with 10 cubes in each.

✤ Sort them into 2 sets, those that are symmetrical and those that are not.

✤ Where is the plane of symmetry?

✤ Have some shapes got more than one plane of symmetry?

✤ Try making other structures with more or fewer cubes and explore these ideas.

✤ Choose one of your structures and try to draw it.

Cinema visit

Cinema visit

CINEMA	
This afternoon	
STUDIO 1 Film starts 1.30pm Film ends 3.05pm	**STUDIO 2** Film starts 2.50pm Film ends 4.10pm

TIMES EVERY 20 MINUTES FROM 7am TO 11pm

Toni and her friend are going to the cinema. They want to see the film showing at Studio 1.

✤ Which bus would they need to catch to get them there on time? It takes 20 minutes on the bus and the cinema is 5 minutes walk from the bus-stop.

✤ If they want to go and have a burger in the Burger Bar by the bus station in town before the film, at what time do you think they should catch a bus?

✤ What are the answers to these questions if they want to see the film at Studio 2?

♣ Which is your favourite day of the week? Why?
♣ Ask the members of your class which day of the week they like best.
♣ Fill in the chart below.

Name	Favourite day							Reason
	Mon	Tue	Wed	Thur	Fri	Sat	Sun	

♣ Construct a bar chart to show your findings.
♣ What information can you find out from your bar chart?

Name _____

Colours

♣ Make a colour die. Colour each face one of the following colours:

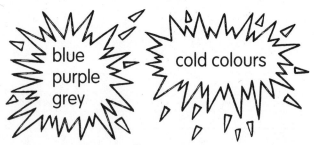
blue
purple
grey

cold colours

yellow
red
orange

hot colours

♣ If you throw the die once, what is the chance of getting a cold colour? A hot colour?
♣ What is the chance of throwing blue? Throw the die 24 times and record the results on the table below.

cold			hot		
blue	purple	grey	yellow	red	orange

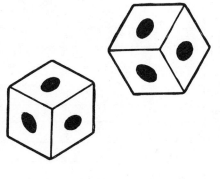

♣ How many times did you throw a cold colour?
♣ How many times did you throw a hot colour?
♣ Is this what you expected? Why or why not?
♣ What would happen if you threw the die another 24 times? Try.
♣ Make a spinner marked with the same colours. Do you think that you will get the same results? Find out.

Name _____

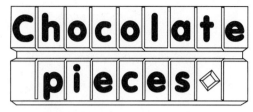

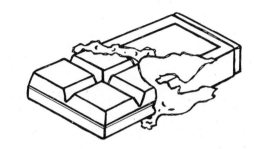

These bars of chocolate have been broken up and mixed up.

♣ Carefully cut out each piece and put pieces of the same size together to make 3 complete bars. All the whole bars should be the same size.

♣ Can you find different ways of making the 3 whole bars by mixing up the pieces?
♣ How would you record your results?

Name _____

Bigger and bigger

Bigger and bigger

❖ Multiply the numbers given below by 10 and by 100.
Fill in the table:

Number	Number multiplied by 10	Number multiplied by 100	Can you predict multiplied by 1000?
3			
8			
20			
32			

❖ Fill in the numbers that have been multiplied by 10 and 100:

Number	Number multiplied by 10	Number multiplied by 100
	20	200
	430	4300
	670	6700
	4800	48000

❖ Fill in the missing numbers:

Number	Number multiplied by 10	Number multiplied by 100
17		1700
	420	4200
	620	
30	300	
	540	

❖ You could make a missing number table for your friend to fill in.

Name _____

New uniforms

The king has ordered new uniforms for his guards.

The first guard's tunic must be $\frac{1}{2}$ red and $\frac{1}{2}$ blue.

The second guard's tunic must be $\frac{1}{3}$ red, $\frac{1}{3}$ blue and $\frac{1}{3}$ green.

The third guard's tunic must be $\frac{1}{4}$ red, $\frac{1}{4}$ blue, $\frac{1}{4}$ green and $\frac{1}{4}$ yellow.

The fourth guard's tunic must be $\frac{1}{8}$ red, $\frac{1}{8}$ blue, $\frac{1}{8}$ green, $\frac{1}{8}$ yellow, $\frac{1}{8}$ brown, $\frac{1}{8}$ black, $\frac{1}{8}$ orange and $\frac{1}{8}$ purple.

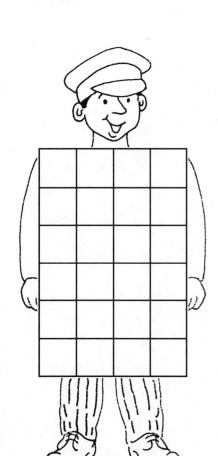 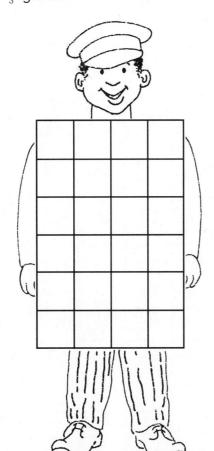 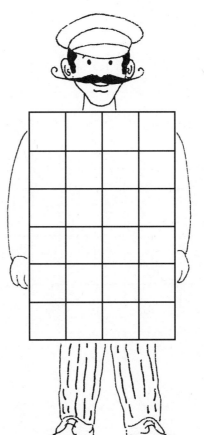 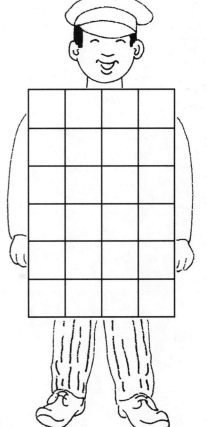

✤ Could you make a different set of tunics for the guards to wear in processions?

Name _____

Which number?

Which number?

There are three different ways to make 4 by multiplying two whole numbers together. They are 1 x 4, 2 x 2 and 4 x 1.

♣ Which number on the hundred board can you make in the most ways by multiplying two whole numbers?

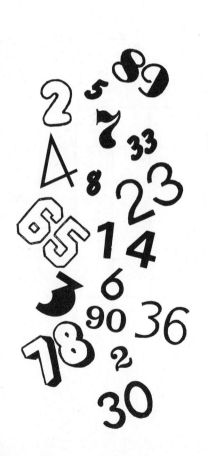

1	2	3	4	5	6	7	8	9	10
11	12	13	14	15	16	17	18	19	20
21	22	23	24	25	26	27	28	29	30
31	32	33	34	35	36	37	38	39	40
41	42	43	44	45	46	47	48	49	50
51	52	53	54	55	56	57	58	59	60
61	62	63	64	65	66	67	68	69	70
71	72	73	74	75	76	77	78	79	80
81	82	83	84	85	86	87	88	89	90
91	92	93	94	95	96	97	98	99	100

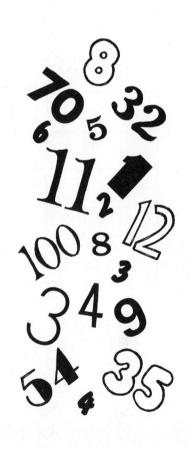

Mathematics

Name _____

Possible products

❖ Using two (1-6) dice, find all the possible products.
❖ How can you classify your results to ensure that all possible products have been considered?

❖ Now try using two (1-8) or (1-10) dice. How will the work you have already done with the (1-6) dice help you?

❖ Use the space below to design a pair of six-sided dice that will give products which include all the numbers from 1 to 17.

Stock check

A shopkeeper has to check the stock in his shop every week. Can you help?
❖ Look at last week's stock list which is shown below.

❖ Now look at how many of each item were sold this week.
❖ Work out how many of each item there are left in stock. One has been done for you.

STOCK LIST (AT END OF LAST WEEK)		
Item	Boxes	Number in each box
biscuits	2	36 packets
coffee	2	24 jars
crisps	10	96 bags
sugar	3	40 packets
choc ices	6	24 ices
dog food	4	36 tins
cat food	5	36 tins
beans	8	36 tins
soup	5	24 packets
peas	4	24 bags

SALES (THIS WEEK)		
Item	Sold	In stock
biscuits	34 packets	38
coffee	15 jars	
crisps	298 bags	
sugar	100 packets	
choc ices	39 ices	
dog food	72 tins	
cat food	98 tins	
beans	200 tins	
soup	100 packets	
peas	48 bags	

Mathematics

Name _____

Can you calculate?

* Three answers are given below for each sum.
* Guess which is the correct answer, then check.
* Put a ring around the correct answer.

572 + 776 = ?   1348   13480   1248

1763 + 359 = ?   21222   2122   4122

5753 + 7742 = ?   16495   13495   133495

1156 - 94 = ?   962   1162   1062

3784 - 1402 = ?   2382   2342   2682

8794 - 363 = ?   9157   5164   8431

* Below you are given some answers. For each one, put a ring round the sum which you think gives that answer.

8876   643 + 8233 or 9639 - 1233 or 2423 + 7453

2546   5546 - 2546 or 6624 - 4078 or 1252 + 1394

5003   1500 + 503 or 233 + 4770 or 2261 + 2942

Mathematics

85

Sharing the bill

Here is a collection of bills from two different restaurants.

A The Peacock Restaurant
Your total bill comes to: £98·42
Service charge not included

C The Peacock Restaurant
£204·86
Service charge not included

D GREENS FISH RESTAURANT
£49·89
service charge at 10% has been added

F
The Peacock Restaurant
£69·51
Service charge not included

B GREENS FISH RESTAURANT
£86·49
Service charge at 10% has been added

E
The Peacock Restaurant
£120.56
Service charge not included

G GREENS FISH RESTAURANT
£149·50
Service charge at 10% has been added

✤ Each bill is to be shared evenly by the following groups of people.
✤ How much will each individual have to pay?

Bill A - 5 people _____
Bill B - 4 people _____
Bill C - 10 people _____

Bill D - 3 people _____
Bill E - 4 people _____
Bill F - 5 people _____
Bill G -10 people _____

Remember
The bills from Greens Fish Restaurant include service charge, but the bills from The Peacock do not. You may wish to take this into consideration when sharing out the costs. When service charge is not included people usually leave a tip. You will have to decide how much to leave.

Matching the pairs

♣ Work out the answers to the sums below. Draw lines to join the sums that give the same answer.

4 x 32   4 x 4

2 x 8   6 x 9

6 x 18   25 x 12

50 x 6   3 x 46

6 x 23   8 x 16

2 x 27   2 x 54

♣ Make up 2 pairs for yourself.

◯   ◯

◯   ◯

♣ Now look at this: 15 x 8 = 30 x 4 = 60 x 2 = 120 x 1

♣ Can you explore the following products in the same way, so that they end with something multiplied by 1?
14 x 8
17 x 6

Name _____

Square numbers

Square numbers

✤ Complete this square number pattern up to 10 x 10.

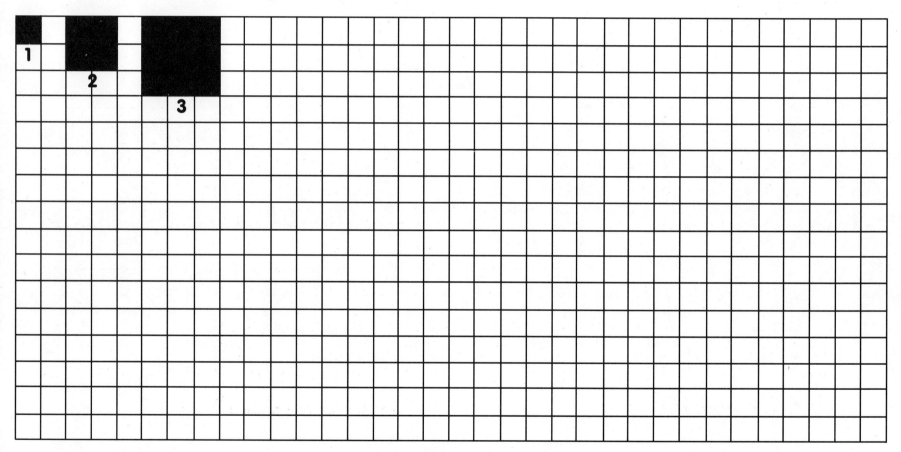

✤ Write out the sequence of square numbers and explore the pattern of differences between the numbers.
✤ Can you see a relationship? If so, explain what it is. Say how it develops and why.

Starting numbers

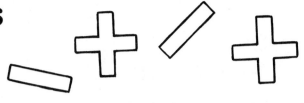

♣ Solve these number puzzles and find the starting number for each.

I doubled it, took away 6, divided by 3 and the answer was 10.	Starting number _____
I multiplied by 4, subtracted 16 and divided by 7. The result was 12.	Starting number _____
I subtracted 12 and divided by 3, then I halved it and added 5. The result was 20.	Starting number _____
I doubled it and added 11. Then I multiplied it by 5 and added 4. I ended up with 89.	Starting number _____

♣ Now try making up some puzzles of your own, check them through and try them on a friend.

Mystery picture

❖ Draw the picture by plotting the co-ordinates and joining each point to the next with a straight line.
1,0; 3,2; 3,5; 3,8; 5,10; 7,8; 7,5; 7,2; 9,0; 7,0; 7,1; 6,1; 6,0; 4,0; 4,1; 3,1; 3,0; join the last point to the first.

❖ Design your own picture. Write down the co-ordinates for it so that someone else could draw the picture from your instructions.

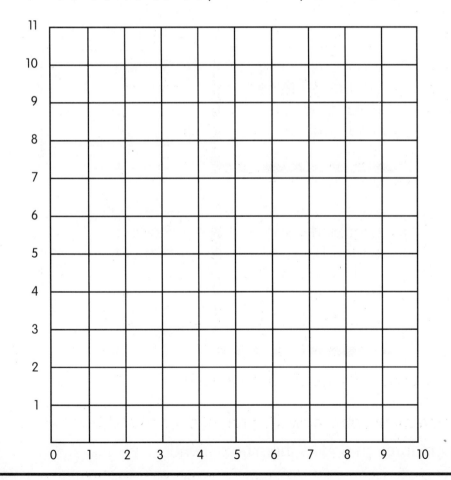

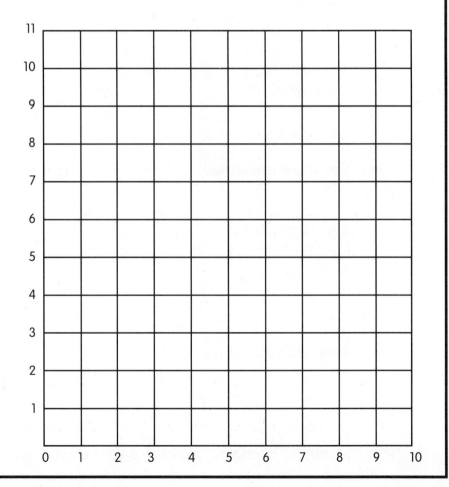

✤ Plot the four-sided shapes given by these co-ordinates.
Shape A (4,1) (5,3) (8,3) (8,1) **Shape B** (10,5) (11,5) (12,3) (10,3)

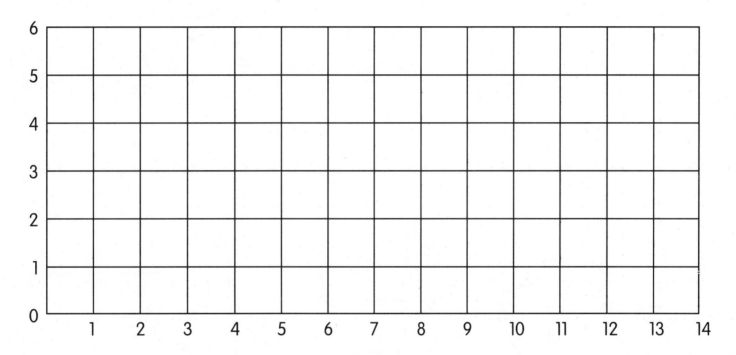

✤ If the sides of each shape are doubled in length, give the new set of co-ordinates for each.
✤ Plot the enlarged shapes.
✤ Work out roughly the area of each shape and make a statement about how the area of each new shape compares with the area of its original shape.

Gold blocks

Gold blocks

♣ Take 240 one-centimetre cubes to use as 'blocks of gold'.

♣ Use centimetre squared paper to make a box with a lid in which to store the 'gold'. Make the box exactly the right size for the gold to fit.

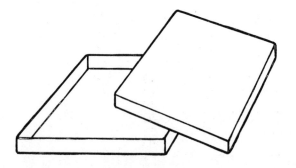
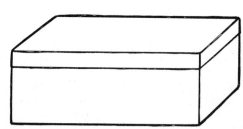
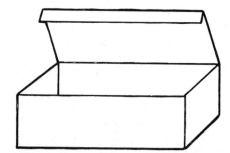

Plasticine weights

♣ Use a 100g weight to make a lump of Plasticine that weighs 100g. Put the weight away.
♣ Now use your 100g lump of Plasticine to help you make lumps which weigh 150g, 200g, 225g, 250g and 300g.
♣ Use your Plasticine weights to weigh things in your classroom.

♣ Find something which weighs ...

between 100g and 200g	_____
between 150g and 250g	_____
between 300g and 500g	_____
between 750g and 1000g	_____

Cubes and cuboids

Name _____

Cubes and cuboids

✤ Look at these drawings and estimate how many cubes you would require to make each cuboid.

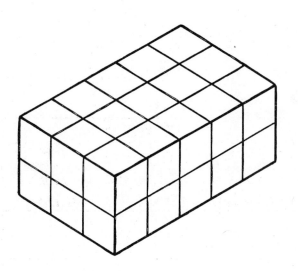
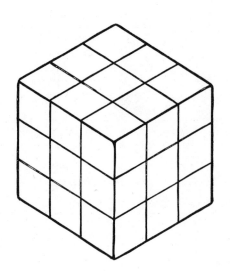
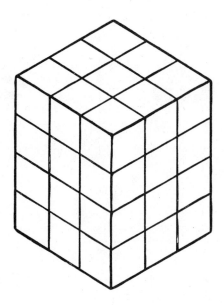

A ——————————— B ——————————— C ———————————

✤ Use cubes to build each one and check your estimates.
✤ Take 24 cubes. How many different cuboids can be made with a volume of 24?

Name _____

❖ Can you write your name in less than 5 seconds? Find out.

❖ Estimate how long it would take you to write out the letters of the alphabet, then use a timing device to check your estimate.

❖ For the following activities predict, before you start, how long each activity will take you. Carry out the activity and time it. Before you check your timing device, estimate how long each activity took. Fill in the left-hand side of the chart.

❖ Now repeat the activities and fill in the right-hand side of the chart. Have your predictions and estimations become closer than in your previous attempt?

Activity to carry out	1st attempt			2nd attempt		
	Prediction of time it will take	Estimation of time it took	Time taken	Prediction of time it will take	Estimation of time it took	Time taken
Read 10 pages of a book.						
Walk around the edge of the hall.						
Run around the edge of the playground.						
Draw a picture of where you live.						
Write the names of all the people in your class.						
Throw and catch a ball 20 times.						
Say a nursery rhyme.						

Angles and lines

Angles and lines

✤ Look around your classroom.
✤ Can you fill in the table by finding two examples of each type of angle or line?
✤ Can you draw a shape using straight lines that has only acute angles inside it? Can you draw one that has only obtuse angles inside it? Can you draw one that has both acute and obtuse angles inside it?

An acute angle	
An obtuse angle	
A reflex angle	
A horizontal line	
A vertical line	
Parallel lines	
A pair of perpendicular lines (other than vertical)	

Name _____

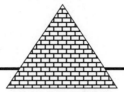

Pyramid

✤ Cut this shape out and use it to make another shape out of coloured paper. KEEP YOUR TEMPLATE TO USE LATER.

You will need:
scissors
pencil
coloured paper
glue

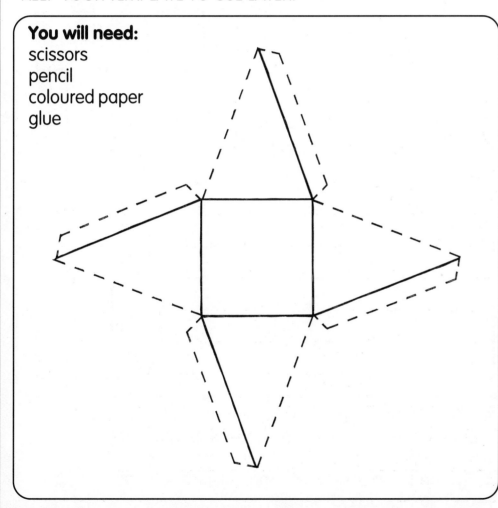

✤ Fold and glue your coloured paper shape into a pyramid like this.

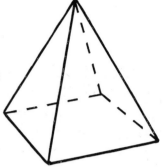

✤ Count how many faces, edges and corners it has and record your findings in the table below.

✤ Use your template to make another pyramid. Join the two pyramids together to make a new shape by sticking the square faces together.

✤ Can you predict how many faces, edges and corners your new shape has? Count them and record the results in the table.

Shape	Number faces	Number edges	Number corners
Pyramid			
New shape			

Rotating shapes

Rotating shapes

Name _____

1   Make the following shape with linking cubes. It does not have to be the same size as the one in the picture.

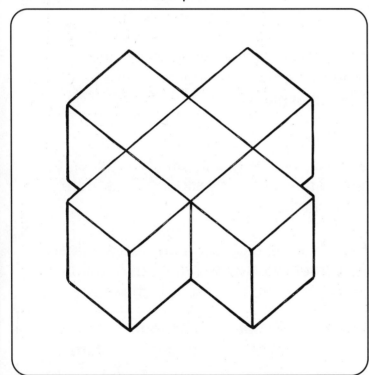

3   Try some more shapes.

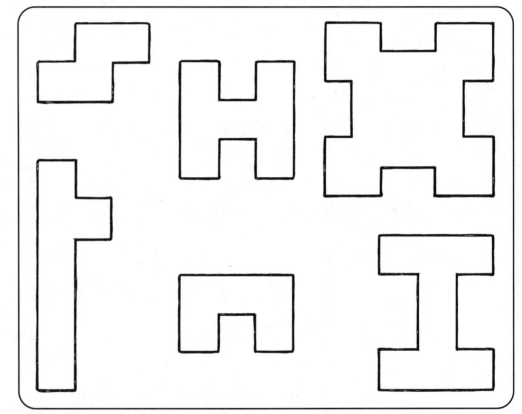

2   Draw round your shape on paper. How many different ways can you fit your shape made of cubes onto your paper pattern? _____

4   Make some shapes of your own with cubes. Draw round them. How many ways can you fit your shapes onto their patterns?

5   Try the same activity with shapes from a set of two-dimensional (2-D) shapes.

Logo designs

♣ Write a program to transfer this drawing to Logo. Test it on the computer if one is available. You could also try to produce each square in a different colour on the screen.

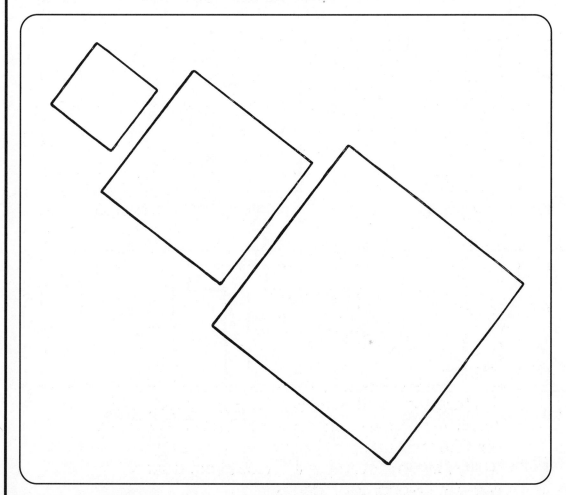

♣ Create your own design and write a program for it below.

Rotation

♣ Look at each shape below carefully and draw next to it what it would look like rotated through the given number of degrees. The first one has been done for you.

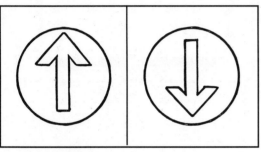

Rotate 180°

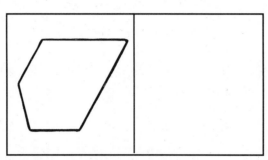

Rotate 90° clockwise

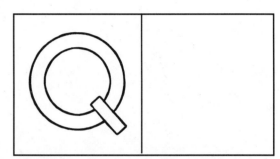

Rotate 45° anticlockwise

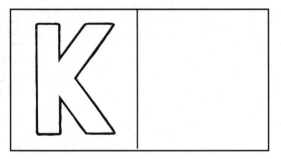

Rotate 45° anticlockwise

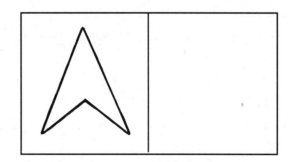

Rotate 270° anticlockwise

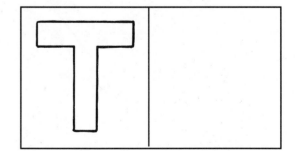

Rotate 270° anticlockwise

♣ Now create some examples of your own for other children to try.

Name _____

❧ What is the average age of the children in your class (in years and months)?

_____

❧ Are you above or below the average age and by how much?

_____

❧ How far above the average age is the oldest class member?

_____

❧ How far below the average age is the youngest class member?

_____

❧ How many, if any, are exactly the average age?

_____

Snacks

Name _____

Snacks

✤ Collect the wrappers from six different snacks and/or sweets.

✤ Make a tree-diagram to sort and identify them. You could start with this question or choose one of your own.

Snacks

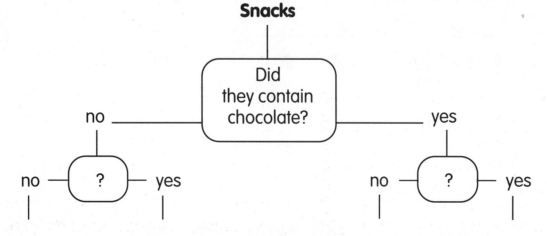

✤ Make a larger collection of wrappers and try the activity again.

Name _____

Watching television

✤ What was the most popular viewing time last night amongst the children in your class?
To answer this question you will need to collect information from each person in the class.
This table may help you :

Time	Number of children watching TV
4:00 - 4:30	
4:30 - 5:00	
5:00 - 5:30	
5:30 - 6:00	
6:00 - 6:30	
6:30 - 7:00	
7:00 - 7:30	
7:30 - 8:00	
8:00 - 8:30	
8:30 - 9:00	
9:00 - 9:30	
9:30 - 10:00	

✤ Construct a graph below to show your results.

✤ Can you suggest why some times are more popular?
✤ Would a similar graph for tonight look the same?

Name _____

Totals

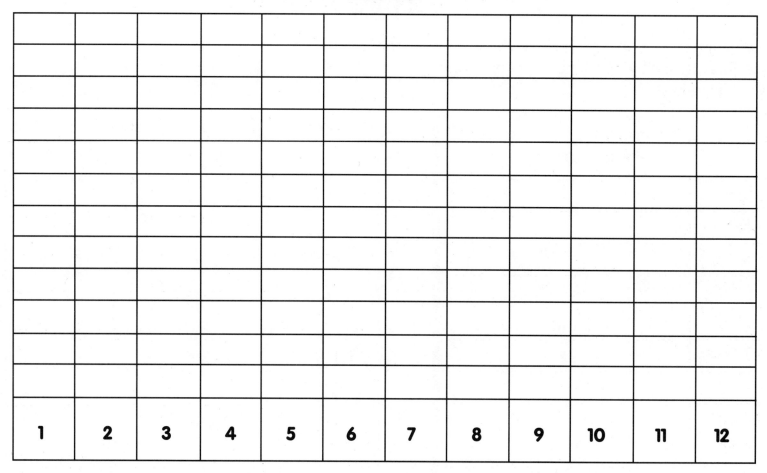

Totals

1	2	3	4	5	6	7	8	9	10	11	12

✤ Throw two (1-6) dice together. Count the total number of spots and tick a box for that number on the table above.

✤ Keep throwing the dice until one column on the table is full. Which number was your most common total?

✤ List all the ways that you could have thrown the dice to get that total.

✤ Using a (1-6) and a (7-12) die, try the activity again. Make a new table to use with these dice.

Drawing to scale

- ✤ On the squared paper below, draw a scale plan of your table or desk.
- ✤ What scale have you used?
- ✤ Using the same scale, draw your possessions on the table.
- ✤ How many times bigger are the real objects than on the plan?

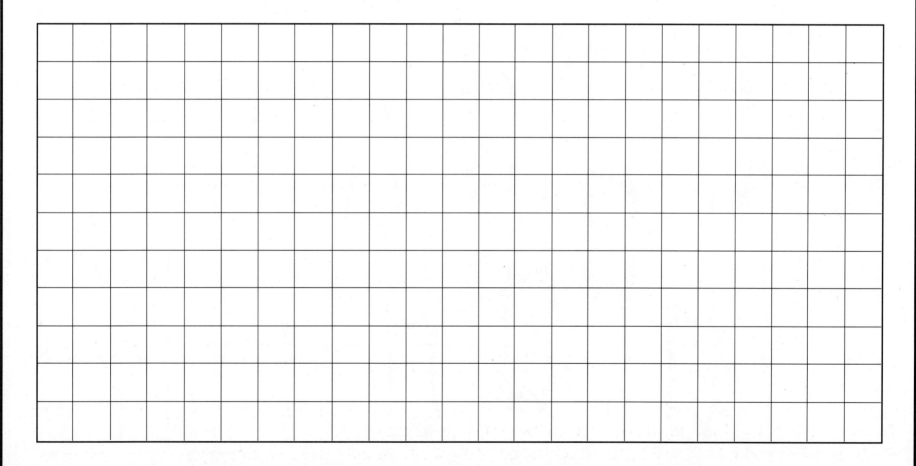

Powers

Name _____

Powers

✤ Draw lines to join the numbers which go together.

125

3 × 3 × 3 × 3

4 × 4 × 4

5³

3³

4

4³

2²

3 × 3 × 3

3⁴

✤ Fill in the table:

2^2	2×2	4
2^3		
2^4		
2^5		
2^6		

✤ Fill in the missing numbers:

3^2		9
4^3	$4 \times 4 \times 4$	
2^3		8
	$6 \times 6 \times 6$	216
		25

Name _____

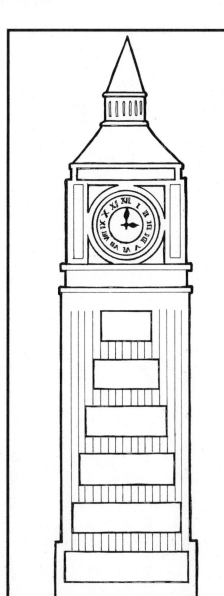

Use your head

♣ Work out the sums below on a piece of paper or in your head.
♣ Write the answers on the towers, the smallest answers at the top going down to the biggest answers at the bottom.

542 x 54   988 ÷ 19

562 x 48   850 ÷ 25

283 x 94   882 ÷ 18

279 x 96   928 ÷ 32

413 x 71   896 ÷ 28

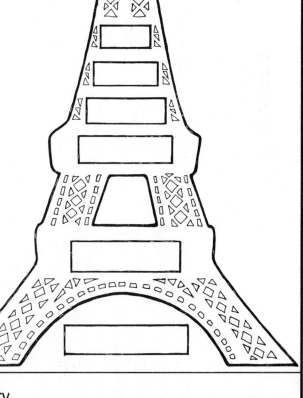

♣ Make up some tower sums for a friend to try.

Name _____

Make it big

| 1 | 2 | 3 | 4 | 5 | 6 | 7 |

Make it BIG

❖ Cut out the numbers on the right.

❖ Arrange the numbers 1, 2, 3, 4 and 5 in any order to give the greatest possible product.

For example:

☐ ☐ ☐ ☐ ☐
_____

or

☐ ☐
☐ ☐
☐
_____

❖ What is the smallest product possible?

❖ Use the digits 2, 3, 4, 5 and 6.
What is the largest product possible?
What is the smallest product possible?

❖ Use the digits 3, 4, 5, 6 and 7.
What is the largest product possible?
What is the smallest product possible?

❖ Is there a rule? If so, can you explain it?

Name _____

Next door neighbours

1	2	3	4	5	6	7	8	9	10
11	12	13	14	15	16	17	18	19	20
21	22	23	24	25	26	27	28	29	30
31	32	33	34	35	36	37	38	39	40
41	42	43	44	45	46	47	48	49	50
51	52	53	54	55	56	57	58	59	60
61	62	63	64	65	66	67	68	69	70
71	72	73	74	75	76	77	78	79	80
81	82	83	84	85	86	87	88	89	90
91	92	93	94	95	96	97	98	99	100

♣ Look at the hundred square. 35 and 36 are next door neighbours.
If you multiply 35 by 36 you get 1260.
We write it like this: $35 \times 36 = 1260$ or $1260 = 35 \times 36$

♣ Which pairs of next door neighbours on the hundred square, when multiplied together, give the following answers?

306 = _____ × _____

2970 = _____ × _____

6320 = _____ × _____

8556 = _____ × _____

702 = _____ × _____

Name _____

How close can you get?

✤ What **whole number** does each of these numbers have to be multiplied by to get as close as possible to 100?

29

14

18

12

34

✤ Use decimals to get closer still. How close can you get?

Use your calculator to help

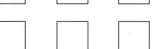

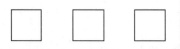

Name _____

Triangles and squares

❖ Represent the triangular numbers under 40 on the squared paper below. Three have been done for you.
❖ Now cut each one out and try fitting pairs together to make squares. What do you discover?
❖ Is there a rule? If so, can you explain it?

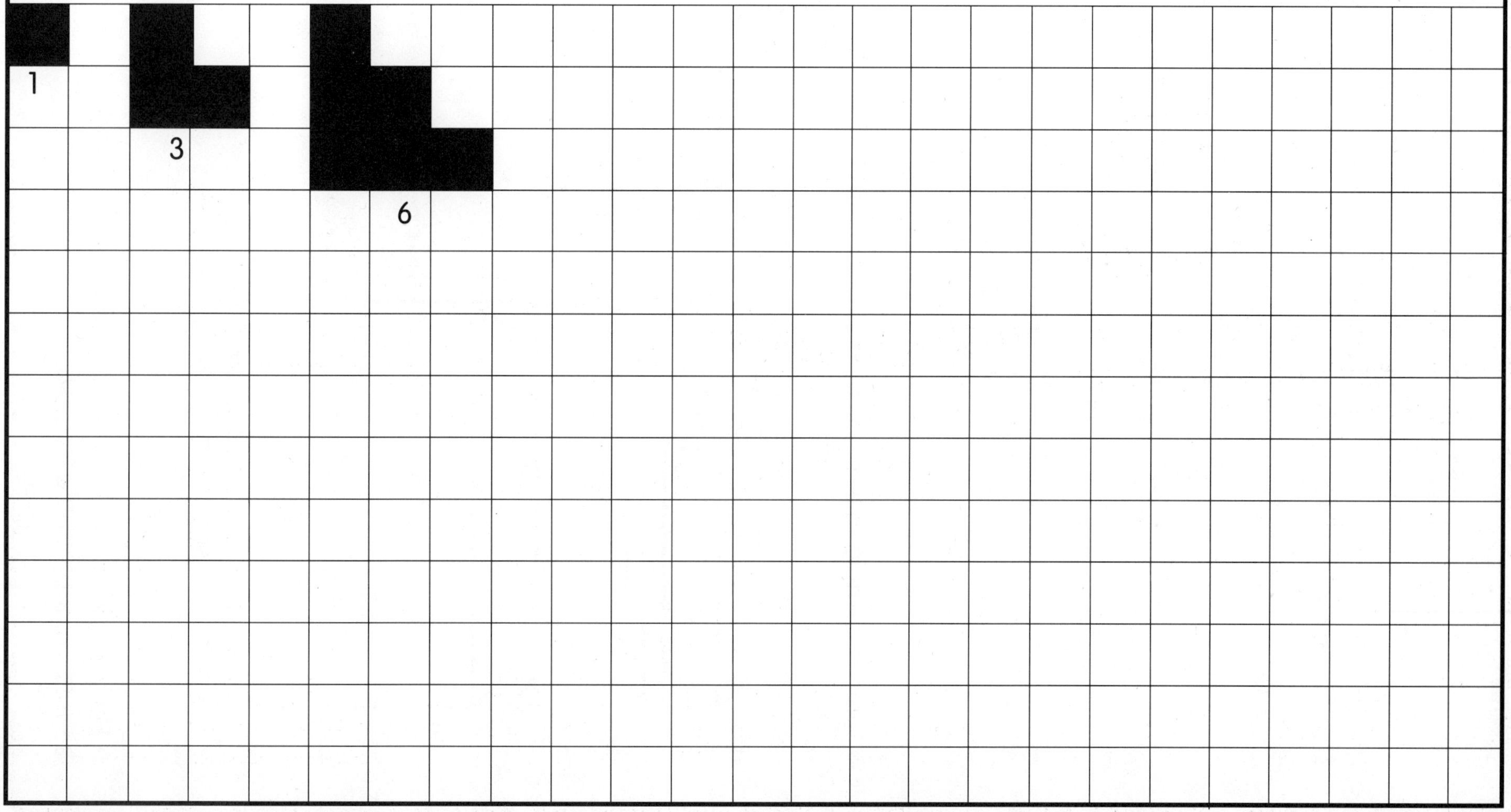

1

3

6

Find the formula

Find the formula

The volume of a cube of side n is given as n^3.
♣ By using the cubes below as an example, explain how this formula is achieved.

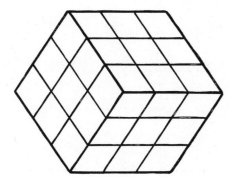

♣ Work out the volume of these cuboids.
♣ Write a formula to express the volume of any cuboid.

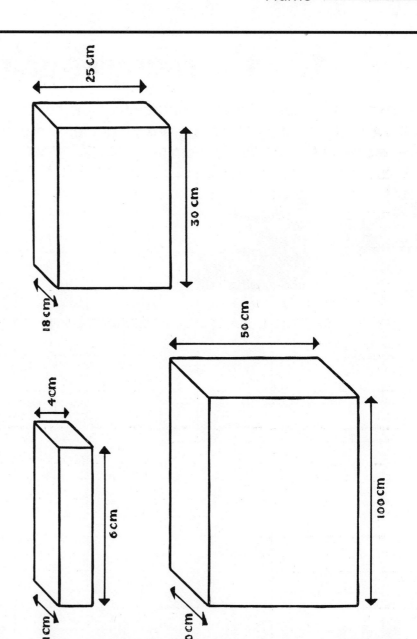

25 cm

30 cm

18 cm

4 cm

6 cm

1 cm

50 cm

100 cm

30 cm

♣ How would you calculate the surface area of each shape?
♣ Write an appropriate formula.

Name _____

Plotting

❖ Write the set of co-ordinates for plotting the boat shape.
❖ Use the other piece of squared paper below to construct one or two shapes of your own.
❖ List the co-ordinates for your shapes on separate pieces of paper.
❖ Give one set to a friend to plot. Does his or her finished product look exactly like your original? If not, why not?

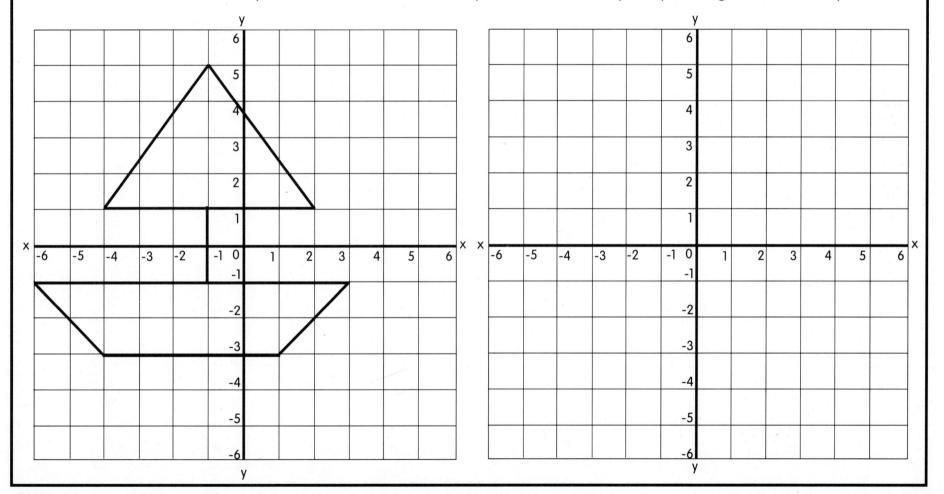

Mathematics

Co-ordinates

Name _____

Co-ordinates

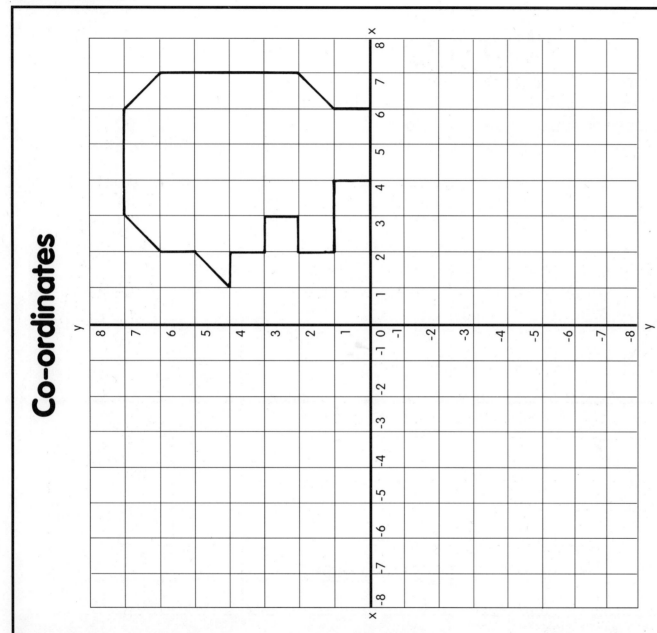

✤ Using the x and y axes as your lines of symmetry draw the head in the other three quadrants so that you have a symmetrical picture.

✤ Write down the co-ordinates of the shapes you have drawn so that someone else could draw a picture like yours without having to see it.

Mathematics

Openings

This is an angle of 90°.
It is also known as a 'right angle'.

✤ Do you have to turn the classroom door handle less than, exactly or more than 90° to open the door?

✤ Could you describe the angle made between the closed door and the fully open door?

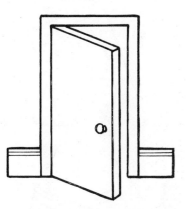

✤ Look around your school at the way the windows open. Can their openings be described in terms of angles?

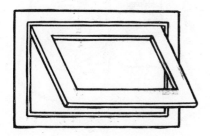

✤ Look around your classroom for other things that open to make an angle.
      How far do scissors open?
      How far do books open?
      Draw the angles that you have found.

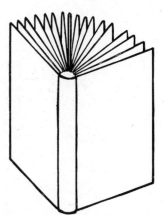

Packaging

Packaging

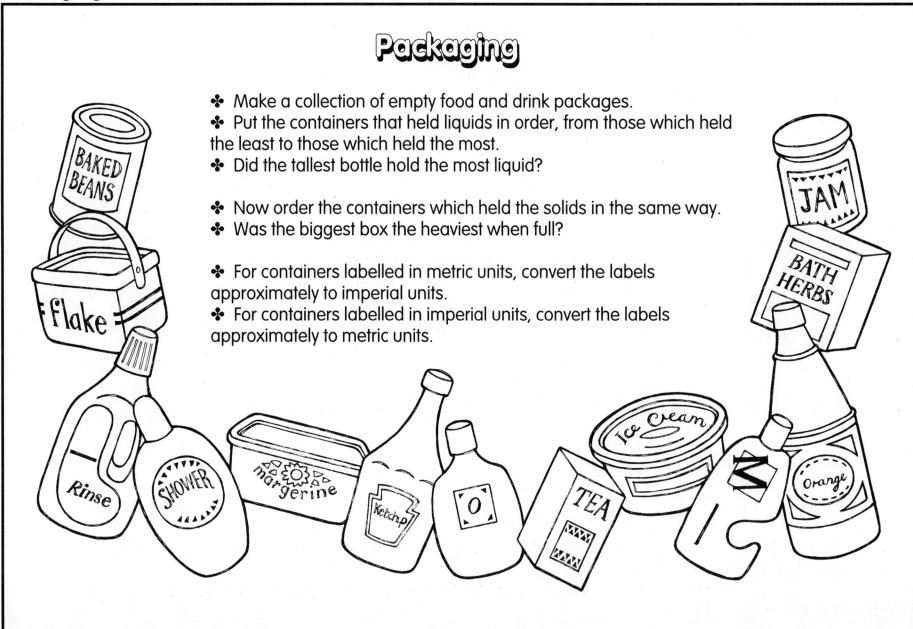

❖ Make a collection of empty food and drink packages.
❖ Put the containers that held liquids in order, from those which held the least to those which held the most.
❖ Did the tallest bottle hold the most liquid?

❖ Now order the containers which held the solids in the same way.
❖ Was the biggest box the heaviest when full?

❖ For containers labelled in metric units, convert the labels approximately to imperial units.
❖ For containers labelled in imperial units, convert the labels approximately to metric units.

Name _____

Snail trace

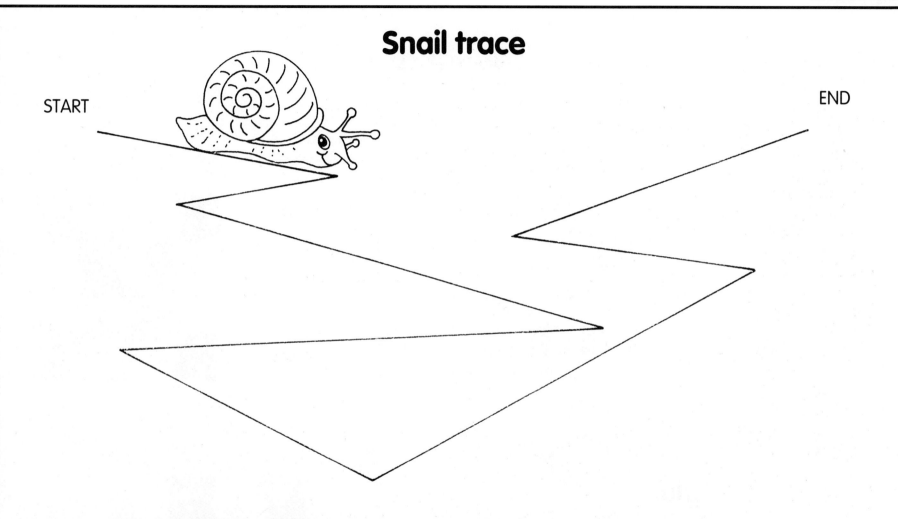

START

END

❖ Give accurate measurements of the distances and angles for this snail's journey.
❖ Using different coloured pens or pencils, draw on two more snail traces and give the measurements for each on separate pieces of paper.
❖ Check your work by asking a friend to draw the traces from your measurements. How do the final results match up?

Name _____

Flooring

Flooring

❖ A kitchen is rectangular in shape and measures 5 metres long and 3 metres wide.

❖ Design a tile pattern for the kitchen floor using tiles in four colours: white, red, blue and yellow.

❖ The tiles to be used are square, measuring 25 centimetres by 25 centimetres.

❖ Draw a scale plan of your design.

❖ Cost out your design.
  - Red tiles £1.10 each.
  - Yellow tiles £1.30 each.
  - Blue tiles £1.20 each.
  - White tiles £1.00 each.

❖ What area is covered by each colour?

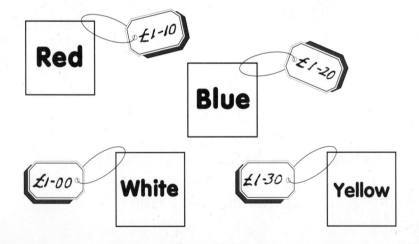

Red £1·10

Blue £1·20

£1·00 White

£1·30 Yellow

Congruent shapes

♣ Colour shapes that are congruent the same colour.
♣ Make two sets of shapes of your own. Include some shapes which are congruent.

Tourist

H – hotel   **C – cathedral**   **P – park**   **G – art gallery**   **M – museum**   **T – theatre**   **Z – zoo**

You are a tourist in this town and want to go sight-seeing from the hotel. On your first day you want to visit the cathedral, the museum and the zoo.

♣ What is the shortest route from the hotel and back again? Do you have a choice? You can only travel along the lines.

On your second day you want to visit the park, the art gallery and the theatre.
♣ What is the shortest route from the hotel and back again? Do you have a choice?
♣ Could you have planned the two days so that you saw everything but did not have to walk so far?
♣ Add some more sights to visit and work out the shortest route.

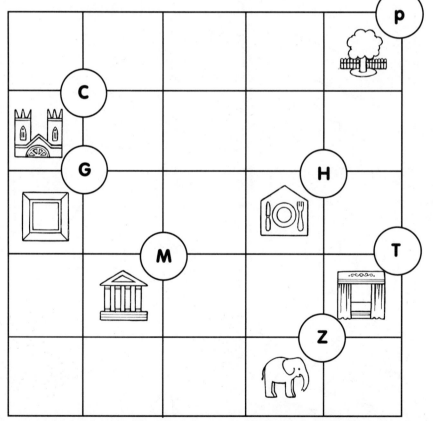

Stop the waste

It is a waste to throw away food.

❖ Design an observation sheet that will allow you to collect information about the types of food that are left and thrown away after school dinners or packed lunches.

❖ Why do you think that this is happening? Make some suggestions as to how this waste might be reduced.

Name _____

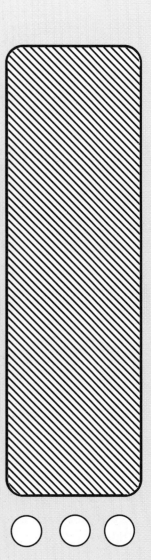

Television times

✤ Do you think there is more sport or more news shown on television?

✤ Which channel do you think devotes the most time to music?

✤ Use a television programmes guide to collect information about television broadcasting for a week. Sort the programmes into categories, for example, sport, music, drama and news.

✤ Work out the average time (in minutes) for each category, shown by each channel, on a weekday and a non-weekday. Present your findings in the form of pie charts. Each chart should show a 24-hour period.

✤ Were your answers to the questions at the top of the page correct? Can you tell just by looking at the pie charts?

Name _____

Recipes

Old cookery books have imperial weights only.
✤ Use the information given to produce a conversion graph.
✤ Now use your conversion graph to help re-write the following recipes with metric weights.

Ounces	Approximate metric equivalent
7	199 grams
4	114 grams
2	57 grams

Treacle treats

4 oz self-raising flour
3 oz rolled oats
1 oz desiccated coconut
4 oz butter
5 oz castor sugar
3 level dessertspoons treacle
1 tablespoon milk

Gingerbread

6 oz plain flour
4 oz golden syrup
1 oz butter
1 oz brown sugar
1 egg
1 tablespoon black treacle
2 tablespoons milk
2 teaspoons ground ginger
1 teaspoon mixed spice

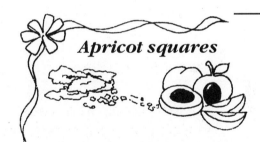

Apricot squares

4 oz dried apricots
3 oz margarine
6 oz wholemeal flour
5 oz brown sugar
2 eggs
$\frac{1}{2}$ teaspoon vanilla essence
2 oz chopped nuts

Name _____

Favourites

Favourites

❖ Write the names of **either** your 6 favourite pop groups **or** your 6 favourite football teams in order of preference in the boxes below.

1		2		3	

4		5		6	

❖ Cut the names out and put them in a bag.

❖ What would be the chances of you picking out your first choice?

❖ What would be the chances of you picking out your third choice?

❖ If you added the names of three more teams or groups, how would this affect the situation?

❖ Experiment and see what happens.

Mathematics

DECIMAL NUMBERS

✤ Cut out the number cards on the right hand side of this page. Deal them into two piles.

✤ Look at the numbers in each set and estimate which has the highest total. Now check your guess.   A calculator may be useful.

✤ Can you make the two piles have equal totals? Can you make them nearly equal?

✤ Shuffle the two sets together and order the cards from highest to lowest.

✤ Make another 4 cards to be included in this pack. The numbers you choose to put on them must be within the range of your highest to lowest cards. Then answer the same questions again.

0 . 14

0 . 35

0 . 07

1 . 03

1 . 13

0 . 71

0 . 24

0 . 98

Jolly jumpers

10% off

¼ off

⅓ off

original price £13·90

½ price

original price £17·60

original price £18·99

20% off

original price £26·50

original price £15·60

All these jumpers have been reduced in the sale.
- ✤ Is the half-priced jumper the cheapest?
- ✤ Which jumper is the biggest bargain?

You have £25 to spend.
- ✤ Which 2 jumpers can you buy and have 1p change?
- ✤ Which is the most expensive jumper?

- ✤ Make up some jolly jumper sale signs of your own.

Name _____

MAIN COURSE
Steak with salad £7.50
Veal escalopes with salad £7.90
Chicken in white wine £6.30
Vegetable cannelloni £5.50
Scampi in breadcrumbs £6.20
Spaghetti Bolognese £5.50

EXTRAS
French fries £0.50
Mixed salad £0.95
Vegetables of the day £0.85
Garlic bread £1.00

DESSERTS
Cheesecake £1.80
Fresh fruit salad £1.50
Ice cream delight £1.80
Profiteroles £2.20

STARTERS
Prawn cocktail £2.50
Lentil soup £1.80
Garlic mushrooms £1.90
Avocado pear and cottage cheese £1.70
Parma ham and melon £2.30

PIZZA
Cheese and tomato £3.00
Mushroom £3.20
Four seasons £3.40
Special £3.60

NB Current prices include VAT at 15% and Service Charge of 10% will be added to your bill.

Sam's Bistro is having its menus reprinted so that all prices include VAT at 17.5% instead of 15% as shown on the menu above.
♣ Work out the necessary price changes for the printers.

♣ Select suitable meals for the following parties and work out their bills. Don't forget that 10% service charge is also added.
• Saturday lunch for a mother and two teenage boys.
• A dinner for two.
• A business lunch for five adults.

Decimal fun!

Decimal fun!

♣ For this decimal game you will need: a partner, a calculator and two different coloured pens or pencils.

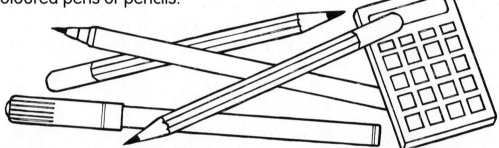

♣ Player A chooses two numbers from the panel on the right and decides to either multiply or divide one by the other. For example 2.3 x 1.2 = 2.76. This is then marked on the number line.

♣ Player B then chooses two numbers and again either multiplies or divides one by the other and marks the answer on the line.

♣ The first player to get three marks in a row, without any of their opponents marks in between, wins.

(If the answer is off the range 1-10, then that player misses a go.)

2.3	**0.17**
5.4	**1.05**
1.5	**7.5**
1.2	**4.2**
0.6	**2.1**
0.8	**6.9**
3.9	**5.3**

0   1   2   3   4   5   6   7   8   9   10

Name _____

S·e·q·u·e·n·c·e·s

❖ Using these starting points, develop a sequence for each and write a rule or formula to express it.

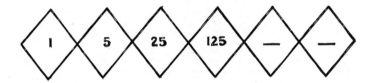

❖ Develop some number patterns of your own. Write the first few numbers in the space below for others to try and find the rule.

Name _____

Soap powder packets

Soap powder packets

A soap powder company has redesigned its packets. The packets are now cubes instead of cuboids and they come in two sizes, medium and large.

❖ Work out the approximate dimensions of each packet.

The volume of the medium packet is 216 cm³.

The volume of the large packet is 9261 cm³.

The packets are packed into larger boxes for delivery and storage. There are 64 medium packets to a box and 27 large packets to a box.

❖ For both sizes of packet, give the approximate dimensions of the packing box, if it is a cube.
❖ Does the packing box have to be a cube?
❖ What shape would be best for lifting and carrying?
❖ Explore different possibilities for each size.

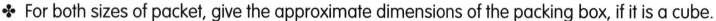

Production costs

This table shows the production costs of a new line of toy.

Number produced	100	200	300	400	500	600	700	800	900	1000	1100	1200	1300	1400
Cost per item (in pence)	50	48	46	44	42	40	38	36	34	32	30	28	26	24

❖ Construct a graph to represent this information.

To meet with a minimum profit margin, production costs of not more than forty pence per item have to be achieved.
❖ Show on your graph the projected effects of production cost increases of (i) 20% and (ii) 40%.
For each increase, use the graph to give the approximate minimum number of items that would have to be produced each time to be within the minimum profit margins.

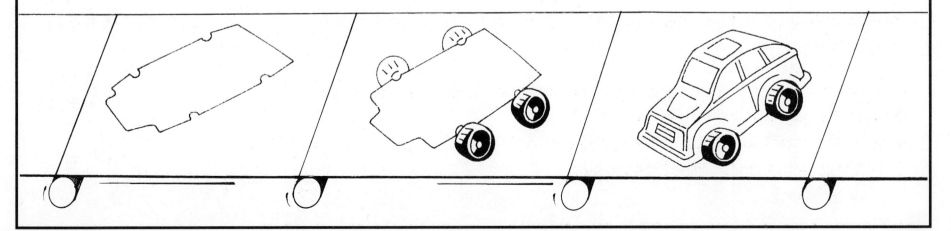

Name _____

Train journeys

Train journeys

❖ Use an atlas to work out the approximate distances, in miles, from London to the cities shown on the map.

❖ Calculate the time of a train journey to each city from the information given below.

Depart London	Arrive	Destination
10.00	14.08	Edinburgh
17.05	19.03	York
12.15	13.35	Bristol
15.35	18.05	Exeter
07.50	10.21	Liverpool

Edinburgh •

York •

Liverpool •

Bristol •

Exeter •

LONDON

❖ Work out the average speed for each journey, assuming that there are no stops on route.

❖ If each train stops at 4 stations for 6 minutes each time, how will this affect the average speed of the train?

Mathematics

Name _____

Va£ue for money

Is buying the largest size always the best value?

Here are four different sized tins of baked beans. Each one is priced.

20p

150g

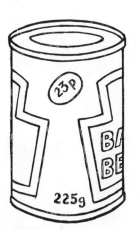

23p

225g

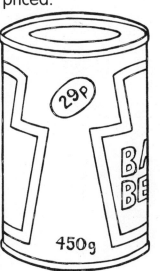

29p

450g

52p

840g

❖ Work out which tin is the most economical buy.
❖ Which is the most expensive?
❖ Were your findings what you expected?
❖ If there was a special offer on the 450g tin and it was selling at 27p, how would this affect your findings?
❖ Carry out some similar investigations on other products.

Tessellating shapes

❖ Do each of these shapes tessellate?
If so, is there more than one way for each shape
to tessellate?

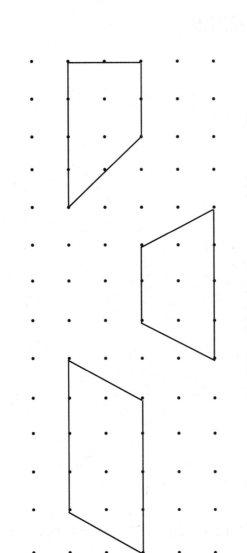

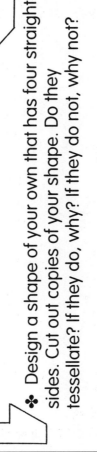

❖ Design a shape of your own that has four straight
sides. Cut out copies of your shape. Do they
tessellate? If they do, why? If they do not, why not?

❖ Do the same for a shape with 6 straight sides.

❖ Try shapes with 5, 7 or 8 straight sides.

Name _____

Tessellations

❖ Cut out the shapes below.

❖ Use each as a template to make more of the same shapes from card.

❖ Investigate ways in which they may tessellate.
❖ For those that do not tessellate, create another shape that will allow you to make a repeating pattern without gaps.
❖ On paper or thin card, construct an irregular quadrilateral. Make copies of this shape and investigate its potential for tessellating.

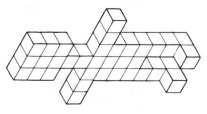

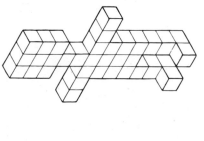

ROBOT

✤ Use cubes to build a simple model robot. Give it a name. Record what you have done in the space below.

✤ Is your picture accurate?

✤ Could you show the picture to a friend so that they could make a model exactly like yours?

Name _____

Designer tiles

A designer produced this bathroom tile.

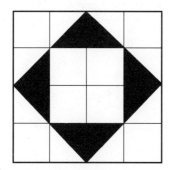

The client liked the design but wanted the length of each side of the tile to be doubled.

♣ On the squared paper, draw what you think the new tile will look like.

♣ How has changing the length of the sides affected the area of the tile?

♣ What would happen to the area if the sides were three times as long as the original?

♣ Could you transfer this design to an area of 36 cm²?

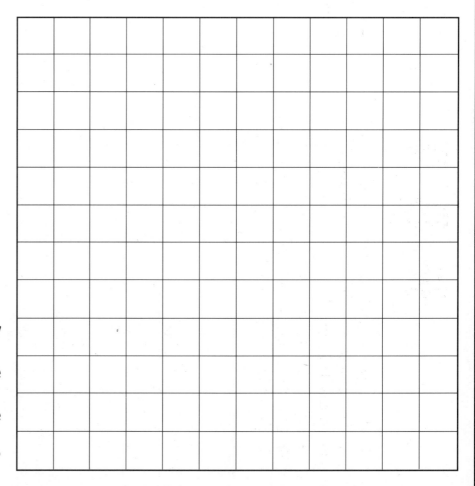

Name _____

Mini-man and Maxi-man

Mini-man
and
MAXI-MAN

This is Mini-man.

❖ Can you draw his brother, Maxi-man?

Here is a picture of his head.

❖ How does the size of Maxi-man compare to the size of Mini-man?

Name _____

Measuring heights

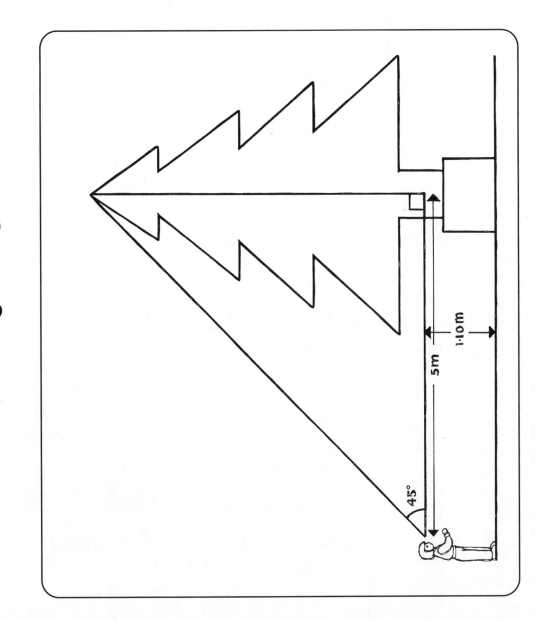

5 m

1·10 m

45°

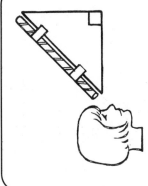

A drinking straw attached along the hypotenuse of the triangle makes sighting easier.

❖ Work out the height of the tree. Don't forget to add on the height from the ground to eye level.

❖ Go into the playground and work out the height of three objects, for example a netball post, a tree and the school roof.
You will need a 45 degree set square – the larger the better – and a metre stick or measuring tape.

❖ Estimate first and then see how close your estimate was.

Guest speaker

Name _____

Guest speaker

❖ If you could have any guest speaker you wished to come and speak at your school, who would you choose? Perhaps it might be an author, a film star, a sports person, a musician or a politician.

❖ Find out who your class would like to have as a guest speaker.

❖ Did the person they chose come from the most common category of people named? For instance, a particular footballer might be the most popular choice, but popstars might be the most popular category.

❖ Ask a class of younger children who they would like as a guest speaker. Find out the most popular category chosen as well as the most popular choice of person.

❖ How would you find out the most popular choice of guest speaker and the most popular category of person for the whole school?

Spoilt for choice!

✤ Imagine that the cook at your school has decided to make some changes to the food served at lunchtimes. Each day there will be a choice of:

Hot meal

Salad

Sandwiches

Fruit

✤ How would you set up a data collection sheet to survey children's tastes and preferences? Remember that you have to take account of special dietary needs and that at least one vegetarian choice should be provided each day.
✤ Use the sheet you have designed to survey your own class. If possible take a wider sample.
✤ Analyse and present your findings. (Your cook may be interested.)
✤ Make up some sample menus based on the results and see how they appeal to your friends.

Name _____

Throwing

Can people with longer arms throw further than people with shorter arms?

✤ Conduct a survey of at least 20 people and fill in the chart.

✤ Present your results as a scatter diagram.

✤ What other factors might affect the length of throw? List some of these on the back of this sheet.

Length of arm	Length of throw

Mathematics

Name _____

Twins

Carla and Wayne are twins.

On Saturday afternoons they can only choose one activity each to do.
The twins might choose to do the same thing or they might choose to do different things.

♣ Show all the choices the twins could make, individually or jointly.

playing with friends

riding a bike

swimming

reading

watching television

playing with toys

Name _____

What are the chances?

❖ If you cut up a hundred square and put the pieces into a bag, what are the chances of:

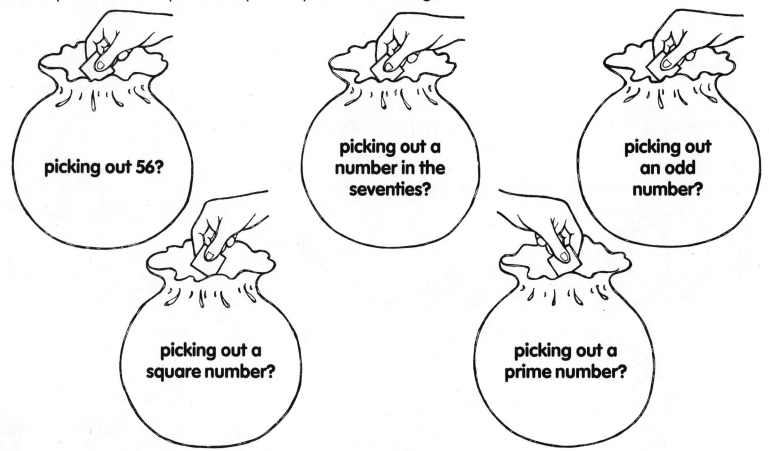

picking out 56?

picking out a number in the seventies?

picking out an odd number?

picking out a square number?

picking out a prime number?

❖ Try to give a reasoned explanation for your views.
❖ If you took out all of the numbers from 1 - 10, how would this affect the chances of each of the above?